J. Mage

The Girl with the Brown Crayon

This book has been awarded Harvard University Press's annual prize for an outstanding publication about education and society, established in 1995 by the Virginia and Warren Stone Fund.

Vivian Gussin Paley

The Girl
with the
Brown Crayon

Harvard University Press
Cambridge, Massachusetts
London, England

Second printing, 1998

Library of Congress Cataloging-in-Publication Data

Paley, Vivian Gussin, 1929–
The girl with the brown crayon / Vivian Gussin Paley.
    p. cm.
ISBN 0-674-35439-7 (cloth)
ISBN 0-674-35442-7 (pbk)
1. Language arts (Preschool)—Illinois—Chicago—Case studies.
2. Children's literature—Study and teaching (Preschool)—Illinois—
Chicago—Case studies.   3. Preschool children—Illinois
Chicago—Books and reading—Case studies.
4. Lionni, Leo, 1910–   .   I. Title.
LB1140.5.L3P35   1997
372.6—dc20   96-34708

Designed by Gwen Frankfeldt

To Irving

Preface

The events recorded here are true, though they seem, in retrospect, something I may have dreamed. Yet how could the children and I, even with our combined dreams, have imagined Reeny's song? "Once upon a time, uh-huh uh-huh, they was a mouse name Frederick, uh-huh uh-huh!" Swish, swish, hands on hips. "Uh-huh uh-huh, I told you so, uh-huh uh-huh, Frederico!"

Reeny is a five-year-old black girl who falls in love with a mouse called Frederick and then makes us think about him and his creator as if everything that happens in school depends on our deliberations. "Guess what, guess what!" she declares. "This is Leo Lionni we doing!"

"Who is Leo Lionni?" visitors ask, looking at the children's giant-sized paintings, each bearing the author's name in uneven print. "Our storyteller," we reply, smiling our secret smiles, knowing that something remarkable is taking place.

And none too soon. Incredible as it seems to me, after more than three decades my final year in the classroom has come. I shall need a miracle to sustain me for the days when my feet no longer carry me to Room 284.

This is my last chance to follow the children into unexplored territory, and never has there been a child so willing to lead as Reeny. How does she know that the whole point of school is to find a common core of references without blurring our own special profiles? Or, to put it into her words, "How come every the whole time I be with one person for a long time they 'mind me of a Leo Lionni somebody?"

"Do I remind you of a Leo Lionni somebody?" I ask, for I have wondered somewhat anxiously over the years about my identification with one of his characters, a bird named Tico.

Reeny studies my face. "He might be not thinking about old people," she says, though the issues in his animal fables she has begun to memorize are ones I have struggled with all my life. Perhaps this will be the year I discover which Leo Lionni somebody I am. At the very least we will have invented a classroom no one has ever seen before, and this has always been miracle enough for me.

In the telling of this literary tale, it may seem that other significant details of school life are obscured by the single-minded dedication of one little girl and her teacher to the words and pictures of a man named Leo Lionni. Stories do proceed as if nothing else is going on, and it is Reeny's story that is told in these pages.

As she herself remarks, " 'Member when I didn't even know Leo Lionni and I didn't even know everyone in this class? That other time got . . . uh, seems like it went . . . uh, somewhere else. And now we got another time to talk about."

"We could talk about that other time too, you know."

"Yeah, but let's us just keep talking about this time."

The Girl with the Brown Crayon

Reeny

The room appears to be filling up with black girls though in fact only Reeny fits the description. "This brown girl that's dancing is me," she says, taping another crayoned figure to the wall. I try to imagine myself telling my kindergarten teacher, "This little Jewish girl dancing is me." The impossibility of my having said such a thing makes me smile.

Reeny's brown girls have begun to encircle the kindergarten. She achieves what is for her the right shade of brown by barely pressing down the first time she colors in the outline, then gradually darkening the tones until she is satisfied.

"Why do you always need a crayon for that?" asks Cory, who prefers markers.

"Because see? It's the same color like me." Reeny lays her hand on the paper. "A marker's too dark."

"Too dark for me too," agrees the very blond Cory, covering Reeny's hand with her own. They became best friends within the first hour of school and begin every day together drawing pictures of girls with enormous amounts of hair. Sometimes

Reeny uses markers for the dress, the hair, or even to outline the body, but the face, arms, hands, and legs are carefully colored in with a brown crayon, which she removes from the box as soon as she sits down. There it stays on the paper, ready to certify: This girl is brown like me.

The two other African-American children in the class are Kevin and Bruce. Today they bring paper and markers and settle across the table from Reeny and Cory. "Gotcha red, gotcha blue," Bruce begins to chant, shaping his big hulking monsters in two colors: red is the good guy, blue the enemy. "Gotcha!" Dash-dash-dash. "Gotcha!" Dash-dash-dash.

The tempo quickens around the table, feet tapping, shoulders swaying. "Gotcha blue, gotcha red, gotcha bad guy in the head. Gotcha this, gotcha that, can't go nowhere 'cause you're flat." Swoosh, descends the purple marker, snuffing out another bad guy.

Reeny moves her head to the beat, but the harmony is not to last. Before long she is at my side. "Excuse me," she says. "I got to tell you something important. Bruce called me a little short-haired black girl."

"And you're—"

"He sayin', '*You* a little short-haired black girl.' He can't say *you* something." She turns to Bruce, who has followed her to my table. "Daddy says if someone botherin' you don't waste time on them, tell the teacher, so I did."

"Sorry," Bruce mumbles, but he is not discouraged. At lunch he calls out, "Hi, baby!" when Reeny passes on her way to get milk. Again she is quick to object, though this time her goal is purely instructional.

"See, I think you saying, 'Hi, baby,' like you saying, 'Hi, girl-friend,' like that? And I'm not your girlfriend."

"Maybe you are," Bruce responds, teasing, but Reeny is persistent. "Uh-uh, see, you can't be. Girlfriend is for very older people. That's for when you grown up. Daddy says 'Hi baby' to my mommy 'cause they already married."

Reeny is not intimidated, as I had been. When I was in the first grade there was an Edward who hissed "Kinky-stinky" at me for my unruly hair, and my face burned with shame. I was too embarrassed to tell the teacher or report the indignity to my parents. Reeny's protests are speedy and decisive.

She is more subtle when I interject a point of grammar during storytelling. "Once there was a little princess," she dictates after lunch. "And a mother and father. They was the king and queen."

"Do you want to say 'They *were* the king and queen'?"

"They *is* the king and queen." She hurries on lest I interrupt again. "And the princess was walking in the forest deeply and she got lost."

"*In the forest deeply* is nice," I offer, to which Reeny says, "Thank you." She knows the difference between literary commentary and personal criticism. "Then the princess sees the opening and there is a prince."

"And he says, 'Hi baby'?" Bruce snickers.

"Uh-uh," Reeny replies with great dignity, "'cause, see, a prince don't talk that way. He say, 'Good morning, madam. How is Your Highness today?'"

She knows what a prince says and what boys and girls should say—and sometimes even what a teacher might refrain from saying. When she talks about herself the message is clear: This is who I am and, so far, this is what I know to be true. How easily she manages her talent for self-identity, something I yearned after but which eluded me most of my life. Not until my forties did I begin to color in the outline, surprising myself by deciding I was a schoolteacher who writes books.

I still cannot take my measure without a classroom of children to give me clues. This year I use Reeny's brown crayon as metaphor, but her role will not be so limited. She is a natural-born innovator and is about to discover an idiosyncratic little mouse named Frederick who will push her into new frontiers.

Where Reeny goes we shall follow. Kindergartners are passionate seekers of hidden identities and quickly respond to those who keep unraveling the endless possibilities. Reeny would be surprised to know that, although grownups are allowed to say 'Hi baby,' they seldom respond as warmly as children do to colleagues whose passions take them to unknown places.

Fortunately, my co-teacher, Nisha Ruparel-Sen, is well versed in the mythology and folklore of her native India and expects the ordinary to open up and reveal mysterious connections. Furthermore, like the children, she is always prepared to enjoy someone else's spectacle even as she creates her own.

Frederick

When Reeny first comes upon Frederick she is wide-eyed with wonder. "That brown mouse seem to be just like me!" she announces, staring at the cover of *Frederick,* a Leo Lionni book Nisha has just read to the class. "Because I'm always usually thinking 'bout colors and words the same like him."

To me, Reeny does not much resemble Frederick. He is a field mouse who stubbornly refuses to help his friends gather food for the winter, spending his time instead composing poems and stories. This shall be his contribution to the welfare of the other mice, with or without their consent. Reeny, on the other hand, is as curious about her friends as she is about herself. Frederick concentrates on his own ideas to the apparent exclusion of all else, reminding me more of myself than of Reeny.

I do not mean to be critical of Frederick, artist and poet, but I do wonder about the lack of guilt he feels toward his friends. He is certain they will remain loyal to him even when he turns away to think his private thoughts. In adult life such loyalty is more problematic. Of course, Reeny is used to the ways of young children, who generally are rather glad to have noncon-formists in their midst.

Having identified with Frederick, Reeny is compelled to in-vestigate further. She takes the book to a table and turns the pages, slowly tracing the mice with her finger. "They so . . . ," she sighs, unable to complete the sentence. But she knows she must learn to draw these mice, to put her brown crayon to the task.

The first picture Reeny copies is of Frederick sitting with his eyes closed under a warm yellow sun, while the other mice struggle to carry ears of corn to their hideout in the stones. ("'Frederick, why don't you work?' they asked. 'I *do* work,' said Frederick. 'I gather sun rays for the cold dark winter days.'")

"He so quiet." In his stillness, Reeny finds her word.

"Frederick's not as nice as them," Cory argues, puzzled at her friend's new interest. "He's being mean."

Reeny touches Cory's arm. "That's not the same as mean. He's thinking. Anyway, those others *is* nicer but I still like Frederick. Look how his tail is, Cory. Don't you love his tail the way it goes?"

"Can you do the eyes for me?" Cory asks, pushing her paper in front of Reeny. I look up to see five children drawing mice; by some unspoken agreement they are following a new cur-riculum.

"I'm not hardly doing eyes yet," Reeny replies. "They the hardest to do. But I'll do it for you but it might not be good. These kind of eyes is the hardest to do."

The eyes they want to reproduce are little dark circles inside larger white ones, simple yet uncommonly tender and kind.

Though Frederick's behavior seems odd to his friends they continue to watch over him with a warmth that creeps into the reader's soul. I wished I could have been regarded this way by the other teachers when my preoccupation with writing books made me seem distant and distracted.

"They do act nice to Frederick," Reeny explains, "'cause they know thinking's not being mean. You hasta be quiet for thinking."

Jonathan calls out from the sand table. "You could anyway think if you're helping!" But Jenny disagrees. "'Member when I had a story in my mind and Mrs. Paley said no because it's cleanup and then I forgetted my story?" Frowning, she waits for my response.

"I'm sorry, Jenny. Frederick's friends would have let him tell his story while they cleaned up."

"You mean *think* his story," Reeny says. "Oh, look here the way he closes his eyes that way." She squeezes her own eyes shut, continuing to draw, but gives up after a moment or two and hands me the book. "Can you read me it again?"

While I read she rubs the textured colors, trying to feel their depth. Frederick sits gazing at the meadow, his back to the others. ("'And now, Frederick?' 'I gather colors,' answered Frederick simply. 'For winter is gray.'")

There are fragments of other colors to copy, a bit of green moss, a reddish acorn, and an orange flower, before Reeny picks up the brown crayon again. Frederick's eyes are lidded, a half-circle of tan across the top. ("'Are you dreaming, Frederick?' they asked reproachfully. But Frederick said, 'Oh, no, I am gathering words.'")

"My crayon is dreaming," Reeny says, marveling at the

lighter-than-ever shade of brown she creates for the eyelids. "Look, Cory! Blankies! You want me to make these blankies for your eyes?" She laughs at her own joke, then holds up the book for everyone to see. "Guess what, guess what!" she declares. "This is Leo Lionni we doing!"

Who *is* Reeny if not Frederick? Her imagery lifts our spirits in the way Frederick's poetry cheers his friends when the food supply is gone. ("'Now I send you the rays of the sun. Do you feel how their golden glow . . . ' And as Frederick spoke of the sun the four little mice began to feel warmer.")

"Uh-huh uh-huh, they Leo Lionni mice." Reeny's song circles the other artists at the table and they respond, humming and da-dumming variations on the original melody. Their smiles flicker like the sunbeams through our gray Chicago windows.

In the course of a morning, the children have taken up such matters as the artist's role in society, the conditions necessary for thinking, and the influence of music and art on the emotions. From Reeny's simple assertion "That brown mouse seem to be just like me" has come a preview of the introspective life.

And I, thought by some to be *too* introspective, though never by Nisha or the children, have met a little girl with a brown crayon and an author with a magic paintbrush who will outshine me in their search for the mirror of self-revelation.

"Who is Mr. Lionni?" a visitor asks.

"*Leo* Lionni," Reeny corrects him. "That's Frederick's . . . um . . . he's Frederick's . . . uh, friend."

Posters

It is clear that Frederick is to remain with us a while longer; were I to know how long and what would be his metamorphosis, I would laugh in disbelief. Yet all signs point to something exceptional; even the multicolored stones on which Frederick sits, quietly dreaming his words and colors, seem to carry a message for the children. "Leo Lionni stones," someone calls them, and they too must be reproduced in their muted autumnal colors.

Reeny insists we need a Frederick poster, "like in the museum," so one morning we push two tables together and cover them with paper from the big rolls in the art room. Then, as directed, I print "FREDERICK BY LEO LIONNI" for Reeny to copy across the top.

When the children arrive they take up brushes and begin a wall of stones with little mice in and around the crevices. By the end of the day, a six-by-eight-foot painting has been left to dry, a panorama of Frederick's world with the sleepy-eyed poet on the highest part of the wall. His eyes are lidded with the tan

color Reeny has been mixing in three separate containers, waiting for the right shade of brown to appear. The color brown, in
all its blends and hues, is important to Reeny.

The poster, now hanging above the piano, dominates my
field of vision, and a not-so-subtle transformation of the common idiom has begun to assert itself. It is Leo Lionni this, uh-
huh uh-huh, and Frederick that, uh-huh uh-huh. In the doll
corner, around the tables, through the sand tunnels, and under
the block buildings, the shapes and colors and words of a single
author have unaccountably put us in rhythm with one another.

But what is really happening? Is it the contagious effect of
one charismatic child's determination to celebrate a mouse as
she celebrates herself? Or do I deliberately engineer this phe-
nomenon because, without something entirely new and remarkable going on, I slip into a classroom half-life? Each year I
wait to be reawakened by a Reeny, just as she has entered
school looking for a Frederick, a *something* to ponder deeply
and expand upon extravagantly.

Oddly enough, when we act out *Frederick,* Reeny decides to
be a mouse friend. "I thought you'd be Frederick," Nisha says.

"The others is nicer."

"You're not like Frederick any more?" Cory asks.

"Yeah, I am, but those other mice love him so much."

How does it feel, she wants to know, when someone else
invents the dance? I am not as brave or curious as Reeny; were
I to join the crowd now I might lose my outline again.

10

Tico

The truth is, I intended to avoid Leo Lionni in this, my last year of school. *Frederick* unexpectedly appeared in a packet of paperbacks, and Reeny immediately brought the book to Nisha to read. Not that I don't admire Frederick; no, my longtime dispute with Leo Lionni concerns another book, *Tico and the Golden Wings*. The behavior of Tico's friends has always been unacceptable to me, and the contrast to Frederick's privileged position is too great for my peace of mind.

Briefly, the Tico story is this: a wingless bird named Tico is loved and cared for by his flock until his dream of having golden wings is granted by a wishingbird. Exhilarated and powerful, he soars heavenward. When he returns to his tree, however, he is in for a shock: his flock rejects him outright. ("'You think you are better than we are, don't you, with those golden wings. You wanted to be *different*.' And off they flew without saying another word.")

How harshly they deal with him. Their anger hurts me as much as it does Tico. This is unfair, I have argued over the years; and, to my dismay, each class has taken the flock's point of view. "He made them jealous!" is the yearly refrain. "He wanted to be too special, he didn't have to ask for *golden* wings."

Poor, undefended Tico. His so-called friends loved him when he was weak, but as soon as he develops in exceptional ways they abandon him. Only when he gives away his feathery splendor to a series of needy people and each golden feather is replaced by a black one do his friends glow with satisfaction and accept him back into the flock. (" 'Now you are just like us,' they said.") Tico is happy and the children are relieved, but I feel betrayed.

Suddenly I must know how Reeny feels about Tico. Surely she, with her brown crayon and her eye for distinctiveness, will defend Tico's right to nurture a special, self-defining quality. I retrieve my own worn copy of the book, abandoned in the closet these past several years, and call the children to the rug. I can hardly wait for Reeny's response.

As we come to the scene where the flock rebukes Tico, the children grow apprehensive. In the flip of a page, Tico moves from euphoria to despair, and the children with him. I can see it in their eyes: Oh, Tico, you must regain your friends' love! When at last his golden plumage is given away and the birds welcome him back, the children sigh with relief. But I am unable to disguise my feelings. "Poor Tico. He could fly so high with his golden wings and see so many things he had never seen before."

"They didn't like it," Jonathan says, to which Cory adds, "He's selfish. Too much gold."

"He could of gave that gold to his friends," Anita thinks, "and then—"

"And to the poor people—"

"And keep two for hisself—"

"But he can't be too special. That's not nice."

One by one the children pluck away Tico's golden feathers. I look at Reeny, who has not spoken yet. "What do you think?" I ask her, unable to contain myself.

She stands to give us her opinion, something she often does when the matter seems urgent. "See, Tico, he gave away all his wings because he wanted everybody to stop being mean to him. But he wanted to have some friends. Because they was being, like, 'I'm not going to be his friend 'cause he has golden wings. And he thinks he's better than me.'" She measures our attention, preparing us for an important statement. "But see, he wasn't really thinking he's better. But *they* thought he was."

I am almost giddy with pleasure. "So, then, his friends were not fair to him?"

Reeny raises her eyebrows, wondering if I understand her. "No, see, Tico he *knowed* they was thinking about that so he took all his gold to give to the poor people so they could have something and then he could have his friends back."

"That was the most important thing, Reeny? To have his friends back? Can't he wish for golden wings and still keep his friends?"

There is a long pause; perhaps she picks up the note of desperation in my voice. Then she smiles at me. "I mean he yes could *wish* for that . . . but not if his friends don't like him anymore. Else he be too lonely."

13

Her explanation covers the subject. Tico is not wrong to wish for golden wings, nor does he consider himself better than others for having golden wings. Nevertheless, once he knows that the flock disapproves, he must accommodate to their feelings. The choice is his to make: golden wings and loneliness or conformity and lots of friends. This from the girl who refuses to blend in yet has everyone for a friend.

"Then what about Frederick?" I persist. "No one asked him to give up thinking about words and colors and be like everyone else."

"They's just different friends," she replies simply. "Tico didn't have that other kind of friends."

"His friends don't care if he's happy," Jenny says.

However, Reeny goes a step further. "They just don't like it if he's *too* happy."

Wings

Journal entry, October 15: "Reeny's social reality overwhelms mine. She takes the question of Tico's rights out of the narrow boundaries I've drawn and insists we consider, quite simply, *the way people are.* Some friends are generous to those who fly off in other directions and some feel deeply offended. On the other hand, certain individuals are more sensitive to the feelings of the group, finding ways to give away some of their golden feathers or perhaps to include their friends more often in their flights of fancy.

"Even so, I would like to ask Leo Lionni why the others needed Tico to be exactly as they are, which is to say, why has he *written* it this way. It seems to me that Tico does not represent the author's personal choices, for how could he have written a single book had he worried about conforming to group standards?"

All of the above is hastily entered into my journal after school. Then, a sudden desire to examine other Leo Lionni books sends me rushing to the library before its doors are locked.

I pull out the Leo Lionni books and pile them on the nearest table. There are at least a dozen including *Frederick* and *Tico*. Passing over the familiar ones, I begin to read *Cornelius* and experience a shudder of anticipation. Has some mysterious force directed me to this book? It is as if Leo Lionni has rewritten Tico's script just to soothe my troubled feelings.

Cornelius submits to no one. He is a crocodile who emerges from his egg walking upright while the others creep along the ground in ordinary reptile fashion. ("'I can see the fish from above!' Cornelius said. 'So what?' said the others, annoyed.") To each discovery announced by Cornelius there is resistance and denial from the community. ("What's so good about that?")

Tico would have dropped down and apologized for his presumption, but not Cornelius. He'll neither capitulate nor compromise, leaving the group rather than accommodate to their jealousy. ("And so one day, Cornelius angrily decided to walk away.") What an independent individual; he is not going to worry about being lonely, come what may.

What is the author's purpose in curbing one hero in order for that character to placate the crowd while propelling at least two others forward? Glancing over the books on the table I try to recall their characters and plots. In each, it seems, there is a struggle between self and community; the conflict is acted out in a dozen different ways. Who do I feel most like, the reader is prompted to ask, a Tico, a Frederick, or a Cornelius? Or one of

16

the other heroes in the collection? And how will my friends react to the choices I make?

This conundrum, which haunts me at faculty meetings and is dramatized daily in every classroom, seems to be Leo Lionni's central theme. If only we could reach into the mind of this mysteriously provocative writer and ask him to explain his work.

As I sit alone imagining the conversation we might have, a practical idea replaces my fantasy. Why not, in a manner of speaking, invite Mr. Lionni (excuse me, *Leo* Lionni) to spend the year in our classroom? He's right here, inside these books on the table. We can ask him anything we wish and, if we become persuasive enough, he cannot withhold the answers.

"Hey, not so fast! What about us?" shout the hundreds of other books surrounding me. "You can't just go off with one author and forget the rest of us!" As if I could ever ignore these old favorites, so rich in language and lore. But surely there is merit in concentrating on a single author, if for no other reason than to discover what happens. The shelves of books glare at me, in the manner of Cornelius's associates, scorning my radical notion. Even the librarian seems disapproving. But no, she simply wants to close up.

Walking home in the dusk, I feel that wings, golden wings, have sprouted and the journey has begun. Reeny has already made me see Tico in a different light, all the more so since I now view him within the context of other Leo Lionni characters. For her, Tico is not the martyr I have believed him to be. He is a perceptive friend who values the flock and empathizes

17

with its feelings. These are not simplistic notions; everyone has a stake in our deliberations.

Is it possible for a kindergarten class to pursue such an intensely literary and, yes, long-term intellectual activity, one that demands powers of analysis and introspection expected of much older students? Why not? I have seen five- and six-year-olds debate their concerns with as much fervor and insight as could any group of adults. Leo Lionni will make the existing intellectual life of the classroom more accessible because he offers us a clear and consistent frame of reference for our feelings and observations.

In any case, Reeny is far ahead of these academic meanderings of mine. "Are you sad about Tico?" she asks me, as we sit on a playground bench.

"It's nice of you to ask, Reeny. I wish his friends were more like Frederick's, or like your friends."

"Frederick told them stories."

"But, you know, Tico might have done that too, after a while."

Reeny looks up at me with her deep brown Leo Lionni eyes. "You love Tico," she says, then skips off to find her friends. They are like Frederick's friends most of the time, eager to hear each other's stories, willing to allow one of their own to soar above the clouds. Yet they too can change suddenly and become as jealous as Tico's flock.

"Last night Leo Lionni came into my dream," Reeny informs us at lunch. "He looks like Frederick, only not the ears. A Frederick person."

don't be afraid to challenge

"So? I had me a Power Ranger in *my* dream!" Bruce shoots back defensively.

"Jasmine came in mine," Jenny says, and Cory recalls that the Little Mermaid was in *her* dream. A wave of resistance ripples around the table. Why should Leo Lionni enter Reeny's dream?

She will not compete. "He was a quiet Leo Lionni. He was thinking. Next time I'll ask him about Tico." The last is said looking at me. Who is this Reeny girl? How does she know that Tico's dilemma and mine are intertwined and must be resolved?

When the children have gone home Nisha and I discuss my idea of a Leo Lionni year. "He's always been a mystery to me," she says. "From the beginning. When I came to this country I was not very much aware of American authors, and I had read very few. I came upon Leo Lionni early, but when someone remarked that he was not for young children, I was confused. I could see the wonderful illustrations, the simple language. I knew it had layers and could go further than young children could understand, but I didn't see any reason why it was not appropriate for young children."

"So, then, did you decide to read Leo Lionni to the children?"

"Yes, I did. You see, we grew up in India with stories from the epic Hindu poem, the *Ramayana*. We called it the great epic. It is far more complex than Leo Lionni's books, but also deals with real human values. Even before I started school, I knew the stories of Hanuman, whose father is Vayu, god of the winds, and his mother a monkey princess. Hanuman is a magical character, a naughty boy and a great hero, a friend of Rama, the king of that time."

"Did Leo Lionni seem pretty straightforward by comparison?"

"No, there are complex abstractions in both. But I think children need stories like these, to bring up their deeper feelings and questions."

"But how do you feel about the length of time I want to spend on Leo Lionni? It is quite a radical notion, you know. I doubt that it's ever been done before at this level."

Nisha laughs. "You have to understand, Vivian, we heard stories from the great epic *every day;* this is why they had such an effect on our thinking. I'm certain that the reason Leo Lionni seems too abstract to some people, and, quite frankly, continued to puzzle me, is that we did not spend enough time with him. One or two books, isolated, are understood only superficially. But *all* of his books . . . now that would be something. I'm all for it, mainly because I want to see how it can be done."

"Okay, then we're both starting out with the same goal: to see how it can be done."

Cornelius

Like the children, whenever I enter new territory I have the urge to make up my own stories. "There was once a little girl who had a brown crayon and she met a mouse named Frederick."

"Did she color him brown?" Jenny asks, smiling at Reeny.

"Yes, and then his friends came, one by one, and said, 'Color me too!' but when Tico came . . ."

"He wanted golden wings!"

"Yes, he did, but the little girl said, 'Sorry, if I color you gold your flock will be angry.' Just then a crocodile named Cornelius walked up, standing tall, looking all around. 'What color do your friends want you to be?' asked the little girl. 'Oh, that doesn't matter a bit to me,' said the crocodile. 'Here, read my book and you shall see.'"

We examine the cover of *Cornelius*. There he is, in several shades of brown, looking proud and happy, walking upright along the beach while the other newly hatched crocodiles crawl about on all fours. ("'I can see far beyond the bushes!" he said. But the others said, 'What's so good about that?'")

"You know something? Jonathan did that to me!" Reeny exclaims before I can turn the page. She looks directly at a surprised Jonathan. "'Member you said, 'What's that stupid thing?' About my daddy's present?" She stands and spreads out her arms as if to gather us all in to hear her story. "See, I was making the present bigger than before, so I was gluing sticks and yarn on the top of the picture, you know the way Cory did that time? And Jonathan was being nasty and laughing and he said it's a stupid thing and a garbage dump. And he didn't say sorry." We look at Jonathan and he says, "Sorry," as if he truly means it.

Reeny, as usual, has brought up her own question and searched for her own answers, producing a parallel to the Cornelius story. Nor is she finished. "See, you was just jealous, but then Mrs. Ruparel-Sen said do you want to show Jenny how to make this kind of present and then Kevin made one too. So I had to make mine bigger to show them how and you kept laughing and making bad faces until Mrs. Ruparel-Sen told you to stop."

No further comments are forthcoming, so I continue reading the book. ("'And I can hang from my tail!' said Cornelius. But the others just frowned and repeated 'So what!'") Disappointed and angry, Cornelius decides to return to the monkey who taught him to hang from his tail and who appreciated Cornelius's tricks.

"You know," I say, closing the book, "it seems to me that whenever we read a new Leo Lionni book, interesting things happen."

"What do you mean?" Kevin asks.

"Just now, for example. There was a problem at the art table and Reeny's feelings were hurt. Then we read *Cornelius* and it tells about a similar thing happening. Of course, Reeny handled her problem in a different way. She told Jonathan how she felt and he said he was sorry."

"The crocodiles didn't say they were sorry," Cory reminds us.

"But Jonathan did, maybe because he could see that Reeny was helping other people. What if Cornelius had offered to show his friends how to stand up? Then would they have been nicer to him?"

Everyone looks doubtful. Jenny shakes her head. "No, because Tico's friends and the crocodile's friends are the friends of each other."

The notion takes me by surprise. "The birds and the crocodiles? From two different books?"

"You're right, Jenny," Reeny says. "See, they always be thinking, Cornelius, he's trying to be better and stuff. They'll always say, 'So what,' like that. It's their habit to do that."

"Friends don't change?"

An unexpected response comes from Walter, at the edge of the rug. He rarely speaks up in a large group. "Books people is have be same," he says, blushing. Later he'll describe the conversation fluently in Polish to his parents.

"But, Walter, can the birds in one book be friends of the crocodiles in another book?"

"Could yes! Could yes! Same is friends. Leo Lionni making friends is same."

"Walter means you could pretend birds or crocodiles but then they act the same." Reeny looks to see if she is correctly representing Walter's ideas and he nods eagerly.

"Very well then," I continue. "Pretend Cornelius and Tico come into Frederick's book. Would Frederick's friends tell Cornelius his tricks are good and would they let Tico keep his golden wings?"

Reeny jumps up and runs to my side. "Leo Lionni could really do that! We could write to him about that!"

"About . . . ?"

"Does he want to change his mind about Tico's friends? Ask him that. Then you'll know. Ask him 'bout that!"

Her determination rules out any note of caution. The children move in closer. Even Oliver, who seldom joins us, comes to the rug. Opening my notebook, I begin to write: "Dear Leo Lionni." Everyone looks at Reeny, who is still standing next to me.

"Tell him Mrs. Paley wants Tico to keep his golden wings. It bother her so much they don't 'low him to do that. And tell him can you please change your mind about Tico?"

There is a hush in the room. Who could have imagined such a letter? Walter walks over to Reeny. "Is good, is good," he says, nodding vigorously.

"Shall we say anything else?"

"Tell him 'cause, see, if Tico's friends got, um, what if *they* wished for silver wings, like that, Tico would just say, 'Oh, great, those is sure nice silver wings you got.'" Reeny rests her case.

After school, waiting for the teakettle to hum, Nisha and I reread the letter to Leo Lionni. "Do you think he'll answer?" she wonders aloud.

"Well, I'll tell you one thing. He's never gotten a letter like this from a kindergarten class."

"Yes, it's a letter that should be answered."

"On the other hand, Nisha, maybe it's not such a good idea to bring the real Leo Lionni into our lives. If he does answer, he may change our perspective in ways we don't want. And if he doesn't answer, the children will feel rejected."

Oliver

"Mommy, come see Oliver!" Reeny pulls her mother through the crowd of early arrivals to a pale blond child hunched over scattered piles of paper. "'Member I told you 'bout his rabbits he's always drawing?"

Reeny knows Oliver won't look up when Mrs. Willens says hello. She also understands that he is not merely drawing rabbits, that he has entered Sha-sha-ma, his private fantasy land, where the inhabitants have begun to organize their story. Bits and pieces of it are strewn about the table. Sha-sha-ma is more real to Oliver than we are.

On one of Oliver's tiny squares, Mother Rabbit pushes Billy Bunny in a stroller; on several other scraps, Richard Rabbit blows up a balloon and bounces a ball or rides on a unicycle. The larger the paper, the larger the story. The page in progress is nearly easel-size: segment by segment Oliver's marker speeds through a fast-paced narrative in which the rabbits watch each other as Oliver never seems to watch us.

Ordinary small talk holds no interest for Oliver. However, if one asks him about any of his rabbits, he will unfold a story complete to its final detail, no interruptions allowed. The children and I watch and listen and wait. Mrs. Willens will soon discover what we already know, that after the calm will come a crisis of despair, bringing classroom life to a halt.

Reeny admires Oliver. She was first to copy his rabbits, even before she fell in love with Leo Lionni's mice. It was she who noticed that Oliver uses one color to a page and will not answer questions that begin with "why."

"Why the rabbits all the time blue today, Oliver?" she asked one day, sitting beside him watching him draw. Receiving no answer, she rephrased her question. "Why you only using the blue marker?" Still there was no reply, whereupon Reeny announced, "Oliver don't like when you ask him *why* something." Months later, a psychologist would tell me the same thing, but Reeny figured it out first.

"Tell my mommy how is Sweetheart doin' today, Oliver," Reeny says, and his response comes quickly. "It's Sweetheart's birthday." Sweetheart and her brother Richard are the central characters in Sha-sha-ma. Good and bad things happen there, but the story usually begins with "Sweetheart and Richard are happy today."

In the brief time it takes Reeny and her mother to pull up chairs on either side of Oliver, the words have begun to flow in waves of precise images. His voice is steady and clear, with no hint of the coming explosion. I should have warned Mrs. Willens, who hangs on Oliver's every word.

"Then Mother Rabbit puts a bow on Sweetheart, tied around her ears, and Richard puts on a new striped jacket." Nothing bad has happened yet, in the story or at the table, but I feel my tension mounting.

Bruce, across the table, is half listening to Oliver and half trying to preempt Mrs. Willens's attention. He wants her to admire his "dangerous volcano," which is about to erupt. As the purple lava bursts forth in larger and larger arcs, a spot of color lands on Oliver's paper. "Oops, sorry," Bruce says, holding his breath, but it is too late.

Oliver shrieks and howls as if in pain. "Ah-ah-ah! No fair no fair he hates me Bruce hates me! Ah-ah-ah, don't look at me get away I hate you I hate you!"

Frantically, Oliver swipes at everything within reach: markers, crayons, paper, and scissors go flying. His sirenlike screams increase in volume as he pushes over his chair and runs for cover behind the carpentry bench. I wish this corner that he always chooses were not so close to the door. His piercing wail can be heard down the corridor, past the third grade classroom, almost to the library. Earlier in the school year, people would run into the hall, fearing the worst, but now they recognize the sounds of Oliver escaping to his hiding place.

Mrs. Willens is visibly shaken. "It's okay, Mommy," Reeny says. "That's his mouse hideout."

We sit silently, waiting for his sorrow to cease. No longer do we chase after him with soothing words and distractions. "No no no get away!" he warns whoever comes near. He begs to be left alone to handle by himself this unexplainable panic that arises out of the most commonplace incidents: a drop of paint on his shirt, a misunderstanding on the playground. "They won't let me! They hate me I'm sorry sorry sorry no fair sorry isn't fair sorry sorry sorry!"

"We didn't say it," the children defend themselves, but nothing will help calm him, except to escape from us. "It can't be somewhere else," Reeny states, whenever the subject comes up, "'cause that's where he goes so that has to be his mouse hideout." Sometimes she is the one at the workbench who has to stop hammering until Oliver is ready to abandon his retreat. Reeny named the place after we read *Frederick,* and the desperate withdrawal no longer seemed so frightening when the corner became "Oliver's mouse hideout."

No one has blamed Bruce, but he is almost in tears. "I don't hate Oliver, I didn't say that," he tells Mrs. Willens, who quickly puts her arm around him. "Of course you didn't, honey," she murmurs, darting troubled looks at Nisha and me.

"Don't worry, Mommy," Reeny assures her again. "He'll be back soonest he can." Mrs. Willens tries to smile, but the frown will not leave her face. I am about to come over with whatever explanation I can manage when suddenly Oliver is back, picking up his paper and putting his finger on the exact place where the interruption occurred. Except for his flushed face and blotchy neck, all is as before.

"I'm sorry I spoiled your picture," Bruce says, but, for Oliver, the event is over. He resumes his narrative in an only slightly less steady voice.

"The rabbits come with presents for the birthday bunny." His finger follows the procession of rabbits, accounting for every item. "Lulu brings a carrot, Betsy brings a striped ball, and Edward Bunny has a lollipop in his paw. Then a bad bad thing happens. A fierce eagle picks up Sally bunny in his talons and she screams and screams."

Does anyone else notice that Sally Bunny's mouth looks curiously like Oliver's when he screams? Not once does Oliver change his expression or look up at his audience when he tells his story. It is as if we are not there. "Mother Bunny hears her child crying and flies up to the nest and pushes out the eagle. 'Don't dare dare *dare* steal my baby!' Then she takes Sally to the birthday and they give Sweetheart a book."

Now Oliver does something quite extraordinary. He takes Reeny's hand and puts it on the miniature book in Sally Bunny's paw. Reeny brings her face close to the paper and smiles. He has drawn a tiny mouse on the book and, above it, the letter F. "Thank you, Oliver," Reeny says, showing her mother the picture of Frederick. "Guess what, Mommy, Oliver is 'minding me of Leo Lionni now."

"Why is that, Reeny?"

"Like, see, he keeps making rabbits, rabbits, rabbits, and see, like, every rabbit knows just what to do and, like, he's not worrying about other stuff, he be thinking only 'bout rabbits, thinking his rabbits all the time, 'cept for now, 'cause Frederick got on his mind 'cause, see, Oliver knows how much I like Frederick."

Mrs. Willens studies her child's earnest face, then looks at those sitting around the table. Finally, she rests her eyes on Oliver, his head lowered, concentrating on a new picture. "I think Oliver is more like Frederick," she says. "And the rest of you are the friendly mice who watch over him waiting to hear his stories."

Oliver has been given many labels but never such literary ones. He is removed from the humdrum of psychological categories and accepted as an artist who concentrates on one thing at a time while we play the role of audience and supporters. How easily Leo Lionni brings us together. Even Oliver cannot escape the net.

Family Stories

Oliver ignores the attention he is receiving, but the literary digression has helped Mrs. Willens regain her good mood. Bruce too wants to reestablish a solid position for himself. He runs to the bookshelf and returns with *In the Rabbitgarden,* the only Leo Lionni book we have that features rabbits. "Look, Mrs. Willens! Oliver draws better rabbits than Leo Lionni." Bruce holds the book open next to Oliver's page of rabbits, careful not to come too close. "See, look, isn't it better?"

Mrs. Willens's eyes travel back and forth from book to drawing paper. "You're right, Bruce. Oliver's rabbits *are* more interesting. Their faces show exactly what they are thinking." Mrs. Willens is excited. "Reeny, look at the mother rabbit's face, how angry she is when she pushes the eagle out of the nest. Oliver, you are a really fine artist."

Knowing there will be no response, Mrs. Willens turns to me. "Shall I do my story now?" she asks. Her visit today has a special purpose, to tell us a story. We urge all the parents to do so, and we particularly like to hear about things that happened when they were children.

"Reeny talks a lot about Leo Lionni lately," she begins as we come to the rug. "Nearly every dinner time we hear something about one of his books. And she talks about Oliver too. In fact, for a while we thought Oliver was a character in a Leo Lionni book."

The children and I burst out laughing, turning to look at Oliver, who sits with his back to us at the little table in the book corner. He does remind me of Frederick, gazing at the meadow, thinking of words and colors. Yet could Leo Lionni put an Oliver into one of his stories, a character for whom life holds so many terrors? Such a book would probably be thought of as unsuitable for children, though the children, for all their frustration with Oliver, do not think him unsuitable for our classroom.

Mrs. Willens continues. "The way Reeny manages to bring Frederick and Tico and Cornelius and Oliver into family conversations reminds me of my baby brother. That's your Uncle Joey, Reeny."

Reeny smiles up at her mother and reaches for her hand. "When Joey was a boy we lived on a farm in Mississippi. He had a pig named Honey he took with him everywhere, except to church, of course. He even took Honey to school, a little bitty school that had big and little children all together in one class. My mother, that's Reeny's grandmother, was the teacher. We all called her Miss Ettie. She didn't mind a bit having Honey for a visitor. She'd even use Joey's pig for math problems. She'd say, 'How can we find out how many miles Honey walks in a week if Joey brings her to school three times a week?' That sort of problem. Or she'd tell us to write a story about Honey or draw her picture.

"Anyway, Joey used to bring Honey into every conversation. Honey this and Honey that. If Joey was asked how the corn is coming up, he'd answer, 'Honey'll have lots of corn this winter.' So one day, Thomas, our oldest brother, got really annoyed at Joey. 'Can't your peanut-head think of anything 'cept that stupid pig of yours?' That's what he yelled at Joey, he was that mad. And our little brother looked Thomas in the eye—mind you, Thomas towered over all of us, so little Joey had to stand on his tippy toes—and Joey snapped back, 'Can't *your* peanut-head see it's Honey that keeps me thinking!'

"Well, even Thomas had to laugh at that one. Our dad was real proud of Joey for figuring that out. Joey was only five or six at the time. Your age. But he knew that if he used Honey for his main line of thinking he could sort of hang a lot of things on that line, the way you all do with Leo Lionni."

Mrs. Willens suddenly realizes that Oliver is standing beside her. She reaches out to touch him, but he squirms away and places a small piece of paper in her hand. On it is a picture of a pig with the letter "S" above it.

"Thank you very much, Oliver," Mrs. Willens says warmly. "And 'S' is for . . . ?"

"Sweetheart!" we all shout together.

It is late, but Nisha and I are still talking. Neither of us wants to leave. "Mrs. Willens has fallen into our net, don't you think?" I say. "She's made the natural connection between Joey's thinking, the way he used Honey and even the way her mother used Honey, and the way we use Leo Lionni."

"Yes, but I think it's more like uncovering layers than falling into a net," Nisha responds. "We've done—what, five of Leo

Lionni's books already? With each new one, plus all the activities that go with it, there is an unfolding of layers of meaning that extends to all the previous characters."

"That's true. We could not understand Tico so well without knowing Cornelius and Frederick."

"I can tell you, Vivian, this is exactly what happens when you are immersed in the great epic."

"When will you tell us some of these stories?"

"Soon, I promise." Nisha has a faraway look. "My mother was a wonderful storyteller. Every night she would have a Hanuman story for us; sometimes I'd ask for the same story night after night, especially if it was sad and made me cry."

Letters

Two form letters arrive, one from Leo Lionni and one from his publisher, both in the same envelope. With mounting sadness, I read them again and again in the middle of the school office.

Unfortunately, Leo Lionni is in ill health and is not able to personally answer letters. We hope you and your students will understand.

Sincerely,
Knopf Editorial Department

The other letter has pictures of mice around the borders:

Thank you for your letter and kind remarks. It makes me happy to know that children and adults as well like my books. It encourages me to go on and make more.

I wish I could send to all my fans a personal note of appreciation. But, alas, time is short and the things to be done are many. I hope you will understand and forgive me.

My very best wishes for happy reading.
Leo Lionni

I think of the box on which Reeny has printed "LLBX," into which has been collected printed messages and pictures waiting to be mailed as soon as we hear from Leo Lionni. "Has the letter come yet?" the children keep asking. What shall I tell them?

On impulse I call the telephone number on the publisher's letterhead. A cheerful, live voice responds in two rings, a good sign. After quickly explaining, I ask, "Can you tell me something about Leo Lionni? The children love him, not in the ordinary way; they love the whole idea of a Leo Lionni. A girl in our class named Reeny even dreams about him."

The woman is kind. "I understand," she says. "Mr. Lionni lives in Italy now. He is eighty-five and not well, but he continues to write. The one time I met him I thought he looked like Arthur Miller, the playwright."

"Ah, with glasses? Reeny dreamed he looked like Frederick, a Frederick person, a quiet man."

"Tell her he *is* a quiet person, like Frederick."

There is a moment of total silence when I read the letters to the children. "You see, he's not well enough to answer all the letters people send him. We're not the only ones who have written to him."

"He won't come," says Jenny. "He's going to die." Her mother died of cancer when she was two. It is not the first time she has come to such a conclusion upon hearing that a grownup is ill.

"I asked him in my dream to come," Reeny says, staring at the box on the piano.

"Let's look at this new Leo Lionni book," I suggest brightly. "Actually it's quite old, but we haven't read it yet. Afterwards we'll decide what to do with the pictures and letters in the box."

Halfway through the book, Reeny begins to cry, soundlessly at first, then in pulsating sobs that reverberate through the room. There are wet faces everywhere. Cory puts her arm around Reeny. "Are you crying because he won't come?"

"We had questions!" Reeny shouts. "We—we—him and us—we didn't—no fair! It's not fair!" She jumps up, still crying, and runs to the mouse hideout, burrowing herself out of sight.

"Reeny, won't you come back, please? You can sit in my lap while I read."

"I don't want to listen! I'm not listening to him!" Then in a softer voice, "Go 'way, Oliver, I don't want you now." Oliver, from some other corner of the room, has heard Reeny and responded to her cry. He squeezes in beside her and there they remain until Cory is sent to tell them it is outdoor time.

Little Blue
and Little Yellow

Reeny takes her crayons and notebook into the doll corner just as we begin the Cornelius poster, and later, when we act out the story, she sits with Oliver, turned away from us.

This worries Cory, who leaves the group to go to her friend. "Are you still Frederick?" she asks, as if she is saying: Is everything lost?

"Don't want to talk about that."

"You could be Cornelius," Bruce calls out from the rug. "He doesn't care if he has friends."

"That monkey is his friend," Reeny reminds him in spite of herself. Bruce and Jonathan have now joined her in the book corner.

The *Cornelius* performance is derailed. It seems that it cannot continue without Reeny. She is our connection to Leo Lionni.

"Hey, know something, Reeny?" Jonathan says. "My mom is really Cornelius. My brother told her he can't practice violin so much because then he won't have any friends. They're all outside playing. So my mom said, 'You better find other friends if that's how they are.'"

"Did he find other friends?" Reeny wants to know.

"Not yet. It only just happened. I don't know if he losed the first friends."

After lunch, I decide to approach Leo Lionni in a different way, now that he has emerged as a real person. Reeny chooses a spot several feet away from the rug, but close enough to see the book. "This is what I began to read yesterday, *Little Blue and Little Yellow*. Did I mention that it was his first book? He was already a grandfather when he wrote this."

Rather comfortingly, it occurs to me that Leo Lionni and I share a biographical fact: neither of us had a book published before the age of fifty. Furthermore, in twenty years, I'll be the age he is now and he is still writing, another heartening thought. "Oh, sorry, children, my mind was on something else."

"On what?" Reeny asks, coming to the edge of the rug. She cannot resist the unspoken thought. "What was your mind on?"

"I was thinking that a person is never too old to write a book. Leo Lionni was a grandfather; in fact, it was because of his grandchildren that he began to write children's books. They were on a train together and the ride was long. To keep them occupied he began drawing pictures—these colored shapes in the book. He called them Little Blue and Little Yellow, and he told a story about them. When he got home, he made it into a book, and people liked it a lot. So from then on he earned his living writing and illustrating children's books."

Reeny moves closer. "What did he do from before that time?"

"He drew pictures for advertisements. And he was good at it, he even got some prizes. But he wasn't happy in that kind of work." I can see that Reeny is puzzled. "Is there something more you'd like to know, Reeny?"

"How do you . . . who told you 'bout everything?" Reeny looks as if she feels she is being tricked. This sudden influx of biographical information must seem even more out of context than the letters from the publisher.

"Oh, sorry, I should have explained. There is a book in the library called *Something about the Author*. It has information about the people who write children's books. I looked up Leo Lionni in the L's. That's how I found out all these things I've been talking about."

I begin to read *Little Blue and Little Yellow* and am surprised to find it is not much to my liking. Two little color splotches, one blue, the other yellow, are playmates. One day, hugging each other, their colors blend and they each turn green, whereupon their families do not recognize them and send them away. The two friends dissolve into streams of blue and yellow tears and each colored shape then becomes itself again. Now they are welcomed back into their families, who somehow realize it is good, after all, to mingle with other colors.

When I first read the book, some twenty years earlier, it seemed a simple, artistic tale, perhaps even a clever way of dealing with the concept of racial harmony. Now the message is confusing.

All the while I've been reading, it is clear that Reeny cannot sit still. She keeps moving around the rug, whispering to herself. Finally, she blurts out, "That's a lie! A mommy and a daddy hasta remember their own child!"

Reeny glares at me, angrier than I've ever seen her. "And you can't neither change colors from hugging! Me and Cory hug and we don't change colors a bit!"

Reeny's interpretation so startles me that I rush to dilute her feelings. "Maybe it's just a story about painted circles, you know, if we mix blue and yellow we get green?"

Reeny shakes her head, wondering at my innocence. "See, they supposed to be *people* circles, else how do they hug?" As she begins her explanation, she grows calmer. "See, if you want colors to hug then you pretend they people. And see, people don't change colors from hugging."

"So he's wrong then?" Jenny asks. "Leo Lionni is wrong?"

Reeny takes a deep breath and stands up. "See, here's what it is. He's old. And he don't—he *doesn't* feel too good. He made a mistake, that's what happened. It's only just a mistake."

"Then do you still like him?" Jenny poses the question on everyone's mind.

"Yeah, I really do." The collected sense of relief in the classroom is extraordinary. A world in which Reeny no longer likes Leo Lionni has become impossible to imagine.

The next day, on our way to gym, Reeny takes my hand. "Leo Lionni won't ever come," she says. "He's too old, like my great-grandma. Old. She can't go out nowhere."

"That's true, Reeny. But you know, Frederick won't ever grow old."

Her face lights up. "Oh, yeah! Oh, yeah, uh-huh uh-huh!" she sings out, skipping around me. "Uh-huh uh-huh, I told you so, uh-huh uh-huh, *Fre-da-ree-co*!"

She grabs Bruce's arm from behind. "Brucie, listen. Uh-huh uh-huh, I told you so, uh-huh uh-huh, Frederico!"

Bruce snaps his fingers. "Cool! Hey, let's do that!" Together they skip down the hall, hand in hand, chanting much too loudly. "Uh-huh! Uh-huh! I *told* you so! Uh-huh! Uh-huh! Frederico!"

My mind is on other matters. Reeny has engaged in a major struggle with Leo Lionni. First, she believes that he has reneged on the promise of her dream; she in turn denies the premise of his first book. Magically, the air is cleared and Reeny resumes the task at hand in a more balanced position. Ultimately, uh-huh uh-huh, it is the *reader* who interprets the writer.

Inch by Inch

We tumbled into the private life of an author and were pulled off course. I should have known better. In college I was taught to study the great thinkers by reading their books, ignoring, for the most part, the details of their lives and the opinions of others. We were to enter into a dialogue with the author, discussing his ideas with the help of a teacher and bringing up questions of our own. In my case the questions did not emerge until much later. Apparently I needed classroom after classroom of young children demanding to be heard before I could identify my own voice and imagine my own questions.

After school I return to the library to choose a book, any book that is not by Leo Lionni, but I find myself drawn once again to the author's biography in *Something about the Author*. As I reread the brief account, a single quotation attracts my attention. Referring to his second book, *Inch by Inch*, published a year after the first, he reveals the meaning of this story about a much put-upon inchworm. "I had to survive and I really made a living telling people things they didn't need to know.

That's what the inchworm did and he managed very cleverly to survive."

I am intrigued. This is the first time I have an authentic explanation of a Leo Lionni book from the author himself. Finding an old copy of *Inch by Inch* on the shelf, I glance through it quickly, knowing now the author's intentions. There is not much to wonder about.

An inchworm (whom I immediately identify as Leo Lionni) convinces a series of birds (obviously the advertisers) not to eat him by offering to measure their beaks, tails, necks, and legs (describe their products in words and pictures). However, when the nightingale insists that his song be measured (when a pushy client demands excessive praise or wants to promise the consumer too much) the inchworm, pretending to measure the melody, inches his way out of sight (Leo Lionni leaves a job in which he feels threatened by the whims of others). There it is, all quite interesting, but one cannot see beyond the author's commentary.

What will the children make of *Inch by Inch,* hearing it only within its own picture context? Will they sense a deeper meaning than the author himself understood, as they did with *Little Blue and Little Yellow* when Reeny was compelled to challenge its message?

It takes only a page or two for the children to see that the inchworm is far more clever than his tormentors. Everyone laughs to see the little worm escape from the nightingale. "But why," I ask, "are the birds so easily fooled? Wouldn't you suppose at least one bird might decide to eat him anyway?"

My cynicism surprises the children. "The birds like him!" Jonathan says. "He's their friend!"

"He's a friend because he measured them in order to save his life?"

Reeny laughs. "They can't be measuring theirself!" She inches her nose along her arm, as if trying to measure herself, but stops before losing her thought. "And guess what? He could've writed down that song too, like my piano teacher does. Except an inchworm can't probably do that."

No, but Leo Lionni might have figured out a way to make the client happy without losing his own soul. And so might I have found a way to measure my colleagues' songs without silencing my own. But if you are a Cornelius or a Frederick, compromise is not an option. Lonely or not, some folks, when required to use another person's yardstick, will simply inch their way out of the forest—or out of the faculty room.

As I examine the enigma with myself in mind, Bruce suddenly sees his own image in the picture. "Yeah, but he didn't *want* to do that stupid measuring! He didn't like to do it and he kept feeling sad!" Bruce sends me a desperate look. "Like when I don't want to do that picture-writing and you tell me 'Try it maybe it'll be fun' but it *never* is. And it always spoils my picture and I can't keep thinking about my picture!"

The book, then, is not about Leo Lionni, nor is it about me. It is Bruce's story. His "gotcha red and gotcha blue" is in danger of being submerged in someone else's arbitrary notions of what is supposed to accompany his pictures. But *I* ought to be wiser than the nightingale. Indeed, I have seen that, for Bruce and several others, the imposition of writing tasks creates anxiety and tension where none existed before. Furthermore, children are often negatively affected when I discount my own observations and go along with the expectations of others.

I give Bruce my biggest smile. "Thanks for telling me how you feel, Bruce. Why don't you hold off on writing, then, until you're ready—you know, until you're curious about doing it. You might even figure out another way."

Bruce returns my smile, and Reeny joyfully pounces on him, singing "Gotcha this and gotcha that, gotcha Brucie 'cause you're flat!"

"Hey, cut it out, Reeny, I'm telling!" But Bruce's eyes are aglow with victory. The inchworm has once again gotten himself out of the forest.

Later, as we walk home together, Nisha comments, "It's taken me longer, I think, than you and the children, but I'm beginning to *feel* these new relationships we have now. When I read *Peter Rabbit* to the class this morning and, yesterday, one of the African folktales about Anansi the spider, the children made connections to Cornelius and to the inchworm. Reeny said, 'But Leo Lionni never thinks someone is naughty.' So I asked, 'What *does* he think of his characters?' This is the sort of question I would not have asked before. I might have thought it was too abstract, but now it seems natural to ask such a question. Anyway, several children had answers.

"Anita said Leo Lionni thinks Tico and Frederick are special. And Arnie said Peter Rabbit is special too, that he could be in a Leo Lionni book. But Reeny really figured it out. She said you have to have a special *problem* to be in his book.

46

"And then, guess what? Before I knew it I had begun a Hanuman story." She laughs at my surprised look.

"Just my luck, Nisha! I'm so sorry I was out of the room."

"Don't worry. Probably I'll keep going. I said that Hanuman seems to me a little bit like Tico and Peter Rabbit and Cornelius and Frederick, all put together in one little monkey prince who also had special problems. What were they? the children wanted to know.

"I told them that some people considered him naughty, that was one problem; another problem was that he had a little bit of magic and wasn't quite sure what to use it for; but the biggest problem was that he wanted to play with the sun. That's what this particular story was about."

"Isn't it a great feeling, tying together all these stories?" I say, as we reach the corner where we part ways.

"Yes, but it doesn't feel as if I'm tying things up. No, it's more like *opening* up, or maybe even discovering things I've forgotten."

Rituals

The inchworm would have found a way to measure the story that Reeny tells today. Indeed, I can almost see him humping along. "Once upon a time, uh-huh uh-huh . . ." She grins at Cory and continues her narrative, pausing now for each "uh-huh uh-huh," but not saying it. "And Tico a bird . . . and Cornelius a crocodile . . . and Ticey a girl . . . they all live together . . . in a house in the woods." She animates the page with tiny brown mice as I write down her words, our hands moving to the same rhythm, two lefties careful not to collide.

"Isn't Ticey your cousin who came to the potluck?" Cory asks. "With lots of braids?"

Reeny nods but does not interrupt her story. "So they all lived together and then a princess knocked on the door 'cause she was lost. 'Can I live here?' 'Sure, you can sleep with me 'cause we're really sisters!' And there was a rainbow."

She reaches over and draws a mouse on Cory's notebook. Cory takes a crayon and taps out "Uh-huh uh-huh," their private joke.

Reeny's singing commercial for Leo Lionni is here to stay, which seems appropriate in a room filling up with Leo Lionni posters; the children have now painted scenes from nine of his books. One of our favorite lunchtime games is to look around the room and call off the titles, in rap style: *Tico and the Golden Wings,* uh-huh uh-huh; *Cornelius,* uh-huh uh-huh; and so on along to *Frederick, Fish Is Fish, Little Blue and Little Yellow, Inch by Inch, Swimmy, Alexander and the Wind-Up Mouse,* and *The Biggest House in the World.*

Sometimes we try to remember the order in which the posters were painted. At this the children do better than the teachers. "Fre-der-ick is number one; Tee-ee-co is number two; Cor-ne-li-us is number three . . ."

The choice of a new Leo Lionni book is fairly random, but we study each one in the same way. We read the book almost to the point of memorizing it, then dramatize, paint, and discuss its finer points, comparing new characters to those we already know and to those in other books as well. The characters enter our stories, our play, and our ordinary conversations.

"Pretend we're lost and I'm Tico, a princess, and then the wicked tuna comes . . ." The giant tuna is the nemesis in *Swimmy;* the children have made him into an all-purpose monster. Jonathan recently ended a story with, "Then the Power Rangers fighted the giant tuna and kicked him into a million pieces."

From first reading to poster can take a week, sometimes two, depending on how busy we are. There are the birthdays, holidays, visitors, and special events, the math, science, and writing, the art, music, and games that we have always included in the kindergarten program. And we make sure to read books by other authors every day. But, for me, Leo Lionni occupies the main stage, alongside the children's own stories and play. I am like Oliver, as described by Reeny to her mother: "He be thinking only about rabbits, thinking 'bout rabbits all the time."

I ask myself: Would I, could I have imagined such a curriculum were it not for Reeny's fixation on Frederick and my equally ardent identification with Tico? Reeny and I are unmindful of the wisdom that cautions "moderation in all things." It is passion Reeny wants: a roomful of dancing brown girls and dreamy mice, mother rabbits who rescue babies from an eagle's nest, princesses who sleep with their cousins and have crocodiles for pets, and friends who color and hug and whisper to each other all day long.

I too require passion in the classroom. I need the intense preoccupation of a group of children and teachers inventing new worlds as they learn to know each other's dreams. To invent is to come alive. Even more than the unexamined classroom, I resist the *uninvented* classroom.

Walter

We hear Reeny running down the corridor on her way back from the library. "Walter! Walter!" she calls out as she enters the room, waving a book. "Look here, Walter, it's the same as you. Get your notebook, boy! I got something here to show you!"

A perplexed Walter searches for his notebook while we crowd around Reeny. She has brought us *Pezzettino,* the Leo Lionni book in which all the characters are configurations of colored squares. The reason for Reeny's excitement is clear: the illustrations for *Pezzettino* closely resemble Walter's drawings.

His notebook is filled with the same connected boxes, which up to now have not seemed to him a cause for joy. In fact, he sees them as daily proof that he cannot draw as well as the others, a burden he adds to his general self-doubts as an English speaker.

"I not can it," he tells me when I ask him to dictate a story or paint a picture. Yet he sits with Reeny talking so quietly I cannot hear what they say; he colors in the outlines of the Leo

Lionni mice she draws for him and listens intently while she "reads" memorized lines from library books. By contrast, he fends off my suggestions as if I am leading him into a trap.

Walter has recently come from Poland. He is fluent in Polish, reading the little books his grandparents send from Warsaw and writing his own thank-you letters. All of this places him well ahead of most of the children in this kindergarten class, but he does not see it that way. Compared to the confident speakers and mouse painters, he judges himself inadequate.

Pezzettino feels the same way. He is a small orange square in a land of towering creatures named after their special skills: the one-who-runs, the flying-one, the swimming-one, the one-on-the-mountain, and so on. "Am I your little piece?" he inquires of each figure, but their responses are evasive, almost accusatory. ("'Am I your little piece?' he asked the strong-one. 'How could I be strong if I had a piece missing?' was the answer.") Finally, the wise-one sends Pezzettino to the Island of Wham, where he tumbles down a rocky hill and breaks into pieces. Collecting himself, he realizes that he too is made of diverse parts and is not merely a missing piece of someone else. ("'I am myself!' he shouted full of joy.")

I am more than a bit annoyed by the haughty, insensitive treatment Pezzettino receives. We'll not even try to include the likes of you, his friends seem to say. We have nothing in common with such a no-talent little square. "Aren't they rather unfriendly to Pezzettino?" I ask. "Couldn't they at least try to find out if he belongs to them in some way?"

"He does belong," Anita says. "They're his grownups."

"His family?"

"Sure," Jonathan adds. "He can't do all that stuff 'cause he's just a little boy."

Reeny agrees. "The tall one hasta be the dad, and the mom is the swimming one. Those others is relatives of him."

"Then why are they so mean?" I ask, but no one seconds my complaint. The family is not mean, they say, it's that Pezzettino is so little. This is *not* a peer-group story, they are telling me; it is about the weakness of the small child in a world of adults, fully developed grownups who are self-sufficient and lack nothing. They do not need little ones to fill in the empty spaces. ("'Do you think I could be wise if I had a little piece missing?' answered the wise-one.")

So then, if Walter is Pezzettino, it must be the teacher who makes him feel inadequate. He plays checkers with Bruce and runs outdoors with Arnie; he allows Reeny to tie a scarf around his head when she needs a prince, and he lets Cory instruct him on how to hold her doll while she's at the sand table. *They* need him. It is with me that he hesitates and falters.

When did I ever properly appreciate Walter's squares? Reeny perceives their artistic integrity, comparing him to Leo Lionni. His "I not can it" is heard when the one-who-teaches comes around. Then he is most like Pezzettino.

Leo Lionni's skill in portraying the feeling of being "less than" is remarkable. Pezzettino is every child who has ever walked into a classroom. "Do I belong here? Does someone care about me?" Perhaps the lonely island Pezzettino is sent to does in fact represent school, where children are broken into pieces in order that adults may observe, label, and classify them. And, having been so dissected, how does the child become whole again?

"Do you suppose Leo Lionni was thinking about real children?" I suggest after reading the book again. "Maybe even his grandchildren, feeling small and lonely in school? I've been wondering if the Island of Wham is something like school."

"It's a rocky place," Kevin reminds me. "How can that be a school because where are the teachers?"

I have known teachers who were like rocks; nothing could move them or alter their ways. Sometimes that teacher has been me. Every path I take these days seems to go inward, to the center of my own memories and regrets. Leo Lionni could have put me in his book as the one-who-remembers, or better yet, the one-with-missing-pieces.

Pezzettino is now "Walter's book." Reeny has willed it so. She and the children draw "Walter's squares" in their notebooks. It is as if he has asked them, "Am I a piece of yours?" and they have replied, "Yes, we need you to make us complete."

I stand behind Walter watching him draw in his notebook. He is copying an odd-looking word over and over until it nearly covers the page. It takes me a few moments to realize he is printing his name, his real name, in big letters: WLADYSLAW.

"How do you say your name in Polish?" I ask.

"Vwahdyswahv," he says softly. "Vwahdyswahv," a bit louder the second time. The "l" is pronounced as "wah," and the "w" as "v." Walter has shown the one-who-teaches a piece of himself. No, he has given me a piece I am missing.

Second Thoughts

As often happens, our discussion of the book proceeds quite differently the next day. We have read *Pezzettino* again and are now acting it out in our new "Leo Lionni way." Today, for example, half of the class, together, in choral style, plays the part of Pezzettino, while the other half, also as a chorus, portrays each of the nay-sayers in turn. A piece of tape down the center of the rug separates the two groups.

The strong-one has just said to Pezzettino, "How could I be strong if I had a piece missing?" when Bruce is moved to explain further. "We wouldn't be so strong if we had a piece missing 'cause then we'd be broken."

Jenny, also in the role of strong-one, takes exception. "We just *think* that. We're afraid to even look to see if we have a piece missing. Maybe we do, Brucie."

Reeny, in the Pezzettino group, crosses the tape to the other side. "You all think you're better than us. Just because you don't have a piece missing. So what if you don't have a piece missing?"

"Okay, I'm changing my mind!" Jenny blurts out. "I *do*

think I have a piece missing! I do! And I'm telling that to Pezzettino!"

Our hero is no longer the outsider begging to be accepted. He is the truth-bringer, who enables the establishment to understand that they need him as much as he needs them. The story has been given its proper ending.

Swimmy

"And it was Tico's birthday so he shouted full of joy." Reeny is on the third page of the story she is dictating. Because today is her birthday she is allowed to go beyond the one-page limit normally set for stories.

"Shouted full of joy," I repeat as I write it down. "That's what Pezzettino does."

"I know. Guess what? Grandma Ettie is telling us a story. When will she be here? Daddy and Mommy can't come 'cause they has to work so my real birthday is at night and Mommy already made the cake and also I helped Mommy make cupcakes for school and why is Grandma so late?" Reeny's excitement is mounting. Her tiny ribboned braids, a new hairdo for her birthday, seem to be fairly shouting for joy as she runs back and forth into the hallway looking for her grandmother.

"She'll be here soon, Reeny," I call. "Come choose the book now." The birthday celebrant not only may tell the longest story but also decides what book we act out, the games we play, and the songs we sing.

"I choosed already." Reeny skips to the bookshelf and returns with *Swimmy*. "I'll be Swimmy," she says, "and everyone else can be the other fish." The role Reeny has given herself is the most heroic in all the Leo Lionni books we've read. However, none of us could possibly imagine how heroic until we hear Grandma Ettie's story.

Swimmy is a small black fish who escapes from the big tuna that has swallowed his friends, a school of little red fish. His courage and determination intact, he finds another school of fish just like the first. They are hiding from the big fish, frightened and helpless. ("'But you can't just lie there,' said Swimmy. 'We must THINK of something.'") He comes up with the best possible plan: he teaches them to swim in close formation, creating the image of a huge fish. ("And when they had learned to swim like one giant fish, he said, 'I'll be the eye.' And so they swam in the cool morning water and in the midday sun and chased the big fish away.")

Reeny's grandmother is a large, affectionate woman. We quickly establish the fact that she and I are the same age. "You'd be a fine kindergarten teacher," I tell her, watching the children swarm about her just as the school of little fish surround Swimmy.

Her laughter fills the room. "Maybe that's because I *was* a kindergarten teacher, plus all the other grades," she says. Ah yes, this is the Miss Ettie who allowed Uncle Joey to bring his pet pig to school. Instantly I picture her in a tiny one-room schoolhouse using Honey the pig in a math problem. It is amazing the way even one story can give someone place and purpose.

When the last cupcake crumbs are wiped away, we settle on the rug in front of Miss Ettie, as we've been asked to call her. "I've been Miss Ettie all my life, it seems, even before I became a teacher. But my real name is Harriet. You know, like my Irene is called Reeny."

"Who's Irene?" Cory asks.

"Who's Irene? Who's Irene?" Miss Ettie looks around as if she can't locate Reeny, then she bends low and swoops her up. "Why, this is my Irene. Oh-oh, I'm embarrassing my baby. Sorry, sweetheart, let's get on with my story. Sit right down here with your friends, baby. This story I'm about to tell is about the real Harriet, the person I was named after. All the children who were ever in my classes knew my story and Reeny has heard the story, but I want all Reeny's new friends to know it too." Her gracious smile covers us all, but her eyes light up whenever she looks at Reeny.

"Actually, I was going to tell another story today, but when I watched the class do *Swimmy* I couldn't help but think about the Harriet I was named after, Harriet Tubman. She was a slave, the same as my grandmother was, and she escaped from the people who owned her, sort of the way Swimmy swam away from the big fish."

Nisha and I look at each other and smile. *Our* Leo Lionni has snagged someone else in his net. I lean forward in my chair with an eagerness to hear Miss Ettie's story that surprises me. After all, I *know* the Harriet Tubman story; in fact, I told it myself in preparation for Martin Luther King's birthday. But this is different. Something else is going to be revealed here, I am certain, that will uncover layers of meaning that seldom are exposed in a classroom. It just seems so odd to me that Swimmy is involved.

Miss Ettie continues. "Then Harriet Tubman did pretty much the same thing Swimmy does. She saved the other slaves, not all of them, unfortunately, but several hundred of them, people who would have been afraid to escape if she hadn't shown them how. One of those slaves she brought to freedom was my grandmother, just a child then. Reeny baby, that was *your* great-great-grandmother, the same age you are now when she and her family followed Harriet Tubman to freedom."

"Did they swim?" Kevin asks.

"Well now, let me tell you, they were definitely not fish. But they had to wade through lots of streams and rivers that nearly came up to their shoulders, carrying the children up high. You see, slave owners used dogs to try to follow them so it was best to cross water often. That way the dogs would lose the scent, the *smell* of the people escaping."

Miss Ettie looks around, wondering perhaps if the comparison to *Swimmy* is confusing. "Now, tell you what, I'll be Harriet Tubman and you all can be the family of slaves escaping. Pretend you've got brown skin like I do, and like Reeny and Bruce and Kevin have. You're tired and sore all over from being worked too hard and beaten if you need to rest or if you want to learn to read and write."

The children flail about in various imagined hard labors: chopping wood, picking cotton, as directed. Some fall down, pretending to cry. Then Miss Ettie whispers, "Pay close attention. Tonight, listen for the hoot owl and then look up for the

Big Dipper. I'll be over there in the woods waiting for you. Sh-sh, be as quiet as you can."

The ceiling becomes a dark, starry sky and Harriet Tubman hoots from behind a tree. Stealthily the slaves follow her through the bushes and trees, balancing themselves, arms held high over the water. Then Harriet throws up her arms. "Freedom House!" she calls softly. "My friends, you have crossed into freedom. Slaves no more!"

Another Layer

As we sit together on a playground bench, Miss Ettie tells me, "When I used to read *Swimmy* to my Mississippi schoolchildren, I'd always point out that he was a *black* fish. I wanted them to understand it will be a black leader who will bring them to a better life and they'd better learn to stick together and help each other."

"Do you still feel the same way?" I ask.

"More so" is her reply. "We had more true leaders in our little colored town, people who knew right from wrong, than I've seen in a long time, black or white."

"Reeny could be such a leader, don't you think?"

"Ah, so you've noticed!" Miss Ettie looks at me in what I feel is a new way. "Yes, indeed she could. It's not just a coincidence she chooses to do *Swimmy* for her birthday book, knowing I'll be here. She knew I'd notice she's the only black girl in the class, so this is a message she's sending."

"What exactly is the message?"

"I believe it's this: Tell me, Grandma Ettie, if I belong here where I'm so different. Or should I still be with my own people like I was in preschool and the way I am in church?"

"Is that your feeling?"

"I'm somewhat ambivalent, but I know Reeny has strong, positive feelings about being black." She waves to a group of our boys who have just run by. "Anyway, her parents really want her in a school like this, in *this* school."

"Well, I'm glad she's here," I say. "Frankly, I don't know what I'd do without her this year. It's my last, you know. I started off with so many mixed feelings, but now, she and I have taken off on this Leo Lionni train ride and everyone has climbed aboard. It's quite remarkable."

"Yes it is," Miss Ettie agrees. "Makes me want to return to teaching." She is quiet for a while, watching Reeny on the slide. The girls have connected themselves together and are racing down in one long screaming chain of daredevils with Reeny at the head.

Miss Ettie turns to me. "Look, I want to be more honest with you. I'm not as ambivalent as I said before. I would prefer to have Reeny in a school with more black children and teachers, in our neighborhood school, for example, which I know is not nearly as good as this one is. But she will not become a leader of her people if she remains here. It won't happen. There are lots of reasons."

Then, in a very determined, almost conspiratorial manner, Miss Ettie decides to give me one of the reasons. "Here is something that happened to my son-in-law the first time he walked into your school, last summer. Steve has put the matter aside, but I can tell you how upset he was at the time. He had stopped off on his way from work to drop off some sort of form for Reeny. He was dressed in his best suit, as it happens, attaché case and all, looking like the successful businessman he is. Apparently he went to the wrong office. There was a young white woman at the desk."

I am staring at Miss Ettie now, not knowing what comes next, fearing the worst as she continues. "The moment the woman saw Steve she pointed to the copy machine and said, 'How long will it take to fix it?' She assumed, no matter how he was dressed, that he was a technician, not a parent. Before he could say anything, another man walked in, a white man, dressed in khakis and T-shirt, and she asked, 'Can I help you?' Apparently the fellow was looking for his daughter's class. There was a summer program going on. Now, as I say, Steve had gone to the wrong office, but the point hit home, even if he prefers now to disregard it. This is the sort of place where a black man will not automatically be assumed to be a parent, as a white or Asian would be."

She waits to see if I am going to respond, then finishes her statement. "This is just one reason why Reeny will not become another Harriet Tubman if she continues in a place where the next put-down is always just around the corner." Miss Ettie stands up to leave. "You see, Vivian, in any black community, Reeny's family are the pillars, the most respected, the leaders."

"Ettie," I say, taking her hand. "I am certain that kind of respect does happen here. But I also think no white person is in a position to argue with you about this. Your story happened here, and there is no way to guarantee it won't happen again."

64

Hanuman

A few days after Miss Ettie's visit, Nisha tells another Hanuman story, and this time I am part of the audience. "When Reeny's grandmother said that Swimmy reminded her of Harriet Tubman, a great American hero, I was reminded of Hanuman, a different sort of hero to the people of India. As I told you, when I was little, *my* grandmother and my mother told me about this monkey prince every night at bedtime. Anyway, the story I'm about to tell is one in which Hanuman organizes the king's army somewhat as Swimmy manages to get the fish to work together."

It occurs to me, at that moment, that a storyteller is yet another kind of Swimmy hero, bringing an otherwise distracted group of people together for the purpose of being lifted up and carried away on the wings of imagery and language. The children and I are akin to that school of little fish surrounding Swimmy, but now it is Nisha who will plan the journey for us.

"A long time ago in India there was a king named Rama. He

had a beautiful princess who was his wife, named Sita. One day a king from Lanka who was a very mean king came in and kidnapped Sita and took her to his land in Lanka. Now, he took good care of Sita because he really liked her and he made sure she was comfortable."

"So what did Rama do?" Jenny asks.

"He was very sad," Nisha goes on. "He did not know what to do. He and his brother Lakshman were looking around for Sita, all over the place, in the forest, everywhere. They were sad and confused. In the forest they met Hanuman, who, as I told you, is the son of Vayu, god of the winds. He said to them, 'I'll help you find Sita.' Rama said, 'How would you do that?' And Hanuman answered, 'I have the power to fly and see where she is.' "

"Does he have golden wings?" Reeny asks.

"You could imagine him that way," Nisha tells her. "Sometimes I imagined wings with sparkling diamonds and rubies. So Hanuman began to fly above the trees. Now, Sita had also been flying above the trees because she had been kidnapped by the wicked king's bird. While she was flying through the clouds she dropped pieces of her jewelry to make a trail."

"Hanuman follows the trail!" Jonathan says.

"Yes, but then there is a big problem. Because you see, Lanka, where the princess is being kept, is separated from India by an ocean. How can Hanuman, who now has the king's army with him, how can they all get across the ocean? Hanuman thinks and thinks, and then he has a plan. If everyone works together they can do it. Each one collects little pebbles and they begin to drop them, thousands of them, across the ocean until

66

a bridge is formed. This way the army can cross over the ocean. Now they are ready to continue their search for Sita."

"Do they find her? I know they find her, right?" The children cannot wait any longer.

"Yes, in the end they do. You are right. But there are many adventures they must have before Sita is rescued. The next time I'll tell you about Hanuman's magical tail that can become as long as he wishes. One cannot tell these stories too fast, because there are all sorts of special things we have to know about Hanuman. We must save them for other stories, so we can think about them one at a time. When I was little I wanted the stories never to end and so I begged my mother to keep telling each one over and over."

Girls and Boys

"That reminds me," Reeny says, during our third or fourth reading of *Alexander and the Wind-Up Mouse*. "Is Willy a boy?"

We look through the book until we find a pronoun attached to Willy. ("One day Willy told a strange story. 'I've heard,' he whispered mysteriously, 'that in the garden . . . there lives a magic lizard who can change one animal into another.'") "Then he *is* a boy," Reeny says. "So why is they all mostly boys?"

"In the Leo Lionni books? Are they?" The children bring our entire collection to the rug. "I've never thought about this before. Reeny says the characters are all boys. Let's see if it is so." I hold up each book in turn. "Tico?" A boy, the children say. "Swimmy?" A boy. "Frederick, Cornelius, Pezzettino?" All boys. And so on. We cannot find any girls.

Walter turns to Reeny. "Girls could be too. Swimmy you was too."

"Walter is right," I say. "You were Swimmy and Frederick

and Pezzettino too. We've been acting out all these books without thinking about boys or girls."

"That's because we do it all together," Reeny replies. "But when I was Swimmy all by myself I thinked about it. Swimmy should be a girl."

"Like Harriet Tubman?"

"Yes," she says.

Until now the question of gender has not come up in Leo Lionni stories as it always does when we act out our own stories. Using our choral method, Frederick, Cornelius, and the others are represented by girls and boys speaking in unison. Not one of the characteristics or issues we've discussed has been perceived as having anything to do with being a girl or boy.

Nonetheless, Reeny has introduced a very contemporary issue. We sit quietly for a few minutes, looking at the posters now covering the four walls, sometimes one above another, almost reaching the ceiling. "I think probably Leo Lionni he wasn't thinking 'bout girls too much because he used to be a boy," Reeny says. Her idea makes sense to everyone.

"And there could be another reason also," I say, reaching for my notebook. "Be patient, now, while I write down these publishing dates: 1963, 1959, 1964, 1960, 1968, 1967, 1970, 1983, 1975. Okay, now, except for *Cornelius* in 1983, all these books came out at least twenty years ago. *Swimmy* and *Tico* were written thirty years ago. In those days, many writers automatically made their main characters boys even when they could just as easily have been a girl."

No one has anything to say. With my notebook perched on the piano and all the dates showing, the subject has become unclear. "Well, let me ask you," I say, pointing to the posters, "do any of these characters *have* to be a boy?"

"Alexander has to be a boy!" Jenny calls out. "Because he's always chased with a broom." All the children nod in agreement. Now that the girl-boy issue has been raised, the stereotype of the "naughty boy" enters the scene.

Alexander, a free mouse, as the children call him, lives in the same house as Willy, a toy mouse, who is petted and loved. ("All Alexander wanted was a few crumbs, and yet every time they saw him they would scream for help or chase him with a broom.") The story ends with Alexander helping Willy become a real mouse by wishing on a purple pebble, but the punishment image sticks to Alexander and thus makes him, of necessity, a male.

"Anyway Willy could be a girl," Reeny decides, "because he's on a pillow, like girls is supposed to be. Alexander has to be a boy 'cause he's like sort of bad, I mean they always be—*are* thinking he's bad."

Bruce objects. "He isn't bad. Is bad when you save Willy? Huh? That mother with the broom doesn't like him."

We've strayed somewhat from Reeny's topic: Why are the main characters all boys? "You know, Leo Lionni kept writing books after *Cornelius*," I say. "Why don't we go to the library and see if the newer books have more girls?"

Reeny and Walter go ahead with a note explaining our mission. By the time the rest of us arrive, the librarian hands us a

Leo Lionni book we haven't seen before: *Geraldine the Music Mouse.* "Here's a girl for you," she says.

"What's the date?" Reeny asks, surprising the librarian.

"Nineteen seventy-nine," she says, looking it up. "Why do you want to know?"

Reeny takes my hand. "We got to know everything about Leo Lionni."

Walking back to the classroom, Reeny thinks of a different sort of question, though perhaps not so different after all. "Is Annie a brown girl like me?"

Willy belongs to a girl named Annie whom we never see. "There is no way of knowing, Reeny. It doesn't say." We have not gone much farther when Reeny asks, "Is the lady with the broom brown or white?"

"We never see that person either."

Reeny frowns. "I think the lady and Annie both hasta be white, because see, Leo Lionni likes the color brown. If Annie and that lady, I think it's her mother, if they . . . are brown, he's going to show us that. He's going to want to draw their pictures for us to see."

Geraldine

Geraldine is indeed a girl mouse. ("In the pantry of the empty house where Geraldine lived, she discovered an enormous piece of Parmesan cheese—the largest she had ever seen.") But the rather complex story that follows has nothing to do with gender.

Having found such a delicious treat, Geraldine shares some of it with her friends, who help drag the cheese to her hideout. Continuing to nibble after they leave, she uncovers in the cheese a giant mouse, made of cheese, holding up its tail as though it were a flute. Thereafter, every night, Geraldine is awakened by the sounds of beautiful music coming from the cheese mouse. Believing the mouse to be magical, Geraldine will not allow her hungry friends to eat any more of the cheese, until she discovers that she herself can now reproduce the music.

Unless I am wildly off the mark, the book represents nothing less than the moment at which the muse enters an individual soul. But why make a piece of cheese the transmitter of such nobility? After all, Frederick's gift of poetry is not sculpted from the stones on which he sits, or from the corncob his friends share with him. His art comes from within, as do Swimmy's leadership qualities, Cornelius's physical prowess, and even Tico's dream of golden wings.

I admit my puzzlement to the children. "I can't figure out why the music comes from a piece of cheese, even if it is in the shape of a mouse playing a flute."

"Geraldine is dreaming," several children tell me. ("As it grew darker, the sounds became clearer and more melodious until they seemed to move lightly through the air like invisible strings of silver and gold. Never had Geraldine heard anything so beautiful. 'Music!' she thought. 'This must be music!'")

"But does the music actually come from the cheese mouse?" I ask.

Reeny's face takes on a glow. "That's like when Leo Lionni came in my dream," she says. "See, in Geraldine's dream she was thinking, oh, that's so pretty, that must be *music*. Like Leo Lionni was in my dream, you look like Frederick, you must be Leo Lionni. My mind was on *him*."

"I see. Geraldine's mind was already on music. That's why it entered her dream." I feel an extraordinary sense of excitement. "Boys and girls, listen to this idea I've just had! All of us are like Geraldine. *All* of us are like Geraldine! We all have, inside of us, something only *we* can see and hear. It comes out in our stories, our play, everything we say and do!"

The vehemence of my interpretation produces total silence in the classroom. In a calmer voice, I say, "Leo Lionni might be telling us that we each have our own piece of cheese. We must keep nibbling on it, to see what's inside."

Walter claps, startling the others, who then, one by one, join him in a rhythmic clapping. "A piece of cheese, I told you so!" I sing out in a full voice, surprising myself.

The children scream with laughter to see me get up and begin marching around the room, my arms swinging. "A piece of cheese, uh-huh uh-huh, a piece of cheese, uh-huh uh-huh." Instantly a snake-line forms behind me, winding around tables and chairs. "I told you so, a piece of cheese!" Oliver lifts his head from a corner table and swivels around to watch us, a tiny smile on his face.

Later, at lunch, Reeny asks me if boys play the flute, too. "Are you wondering why Leo Lionni made the music mouse a girl? Yes, a boy can also become a flutist," I tell her.

"He just wanted to let girls have a turn to be someone? That's called a flutist?" Reeny hums to herself as she arranges her lunch box leftovers. "A flutist," she repeats softly on the way to her cubby. "A flu-oo-oo-tist."

There she goes, Geraldine herself, always nibbling away, eager to find what's inside. If cheese is the symbolic substance out of which Geraldine's creativity emerges, then it may be that Miss Ettie has given Reeny the sustaining story out of which to carve her unique talents, among which certainly is the ability to help us recognize who we are and how we are connected.

Cleaning up together after school, I say to Nisha, "I thought of a fancy way of describing what's happening to us this year. *Narrative continuity.* We have discovered another way of achieving narrative continuity."

Nisha puts down the paint jar she is washing and smiles at me. "I think you once told me that *play* is narrative continuity."

74

"That's exactly the point," I reply. "It feels as though we are marching to that same rhythm, as in play, or as you did when you heard the stories from the great epic every night. Now we are putting Leo Lionni to the test. Can he provide yet another vehicle for this instinctive need to concentrate for a long time on a connected set of images and dramatic events? Let's face it, what school usually does is continually *interrupt* any attempt on the part of children to recapture the highly focused intensity of play. What we need to do is help them—and ourselves—get back on the track."

Nisha pours out two cups of tea and motions me to the table she has just scrubbed. "You know what the Leo Lionni curriculum reminds me of?" she says. "It's like Hanuman's magic tail. It can grow longer and longer until it can wrap itself around everything and everybody."

Forgiveness

Reeny has begun to make a collage as a present for Leo Lionni. It is already larger than the one she made for her father but is similar in design. After a half hour of working by herself she invites everyone to participate, and the proposed gift quickly engulfs the table, layer upon layer of paper, cardboard, plastic, and wood, bound in tape and string, overlaid with glue and paint. The word "chaos" comes to mind.

"Mrs. Ruparel-Sen is going to need that table for a math game," I say. "Probably early tomorrow."

"It's not finished!" moans Reeny. She is no longer working on the project, but does not want it to end. She walks around the table gazing proudly at this unstructured communal labor of lovely mess, the unrivaled focus of the room.

"You'll all have to finish by the end of today," is my firm response, "so it can dry overnight." The gift has taken on a dreamlike quality; no one seems to wonder how such a massive structure can be sent to Leo Lionni, far away, in his village in Italy.

Nisha moves us into the block area to continue an ongoing math activity using blocks of different sizes. "Now yesterday we pretended there was a family of ten small blocks, and then along came . . ." Out of the corner of my eye looms the sign of impending disaster. "Oliver!" I cry out. "No! Wait, Oliver, don't sit there! Oliver! No!"

Is it possible he does not see what is on the table? Reaching for a marker, his sleeve meets a glob of purple glue that immediately splatters on his pants as he attempts to shake off the paint.

Gasping in horror, he begins to scream, grabbing the edge of the newspaper and pulling the construction after him like a tidal wave. It misses him by inches and his hysterics increase to a deafening pitch.

Reeny is there before I am. "I hate you, Oliver!" she shouts, shaking his arm, determined to make him answer. "Why did you do that? Bad, bad boy! Why did you spoil everything? You're never going to be my friend! I'm not playing with you, Oliver! Never again!"

His head bobbing in fear, he wrests himself away and runs to his hideout. Reeny does not follow. She begins to weep quietly. I put my arm around her. "I'm sorry, Reeny. I should have warned him. He got so scared when the paint got on him."

"Why is he like that?" Reeny asks, as if realizing for the first time that he is "like that." She sits on my lap and we listen to Oliver, hidden in the corner, still crying. "Sorry I'm sorry sorry don't say you're sorry sorry . . ." His voice trails off into a whisper.

"Reeny, won't you tell him you're still his friend, please?

Oliver doesn't understand what just happened. He'll keep crying if you don't forgive him. Can you do that for him?" She puts her arms around my neck and closes her eyes while I sing to her softly. "Go tell Aunt Rhodie, go tell Aunt Rhodie, go tell Aunt Rhodie, her old gray goose is dead . . ." The children gather around us, sad-eyed and weary.

When I stop singing, Reeny slips off my lap and walks to Oliver's hideout, kneeling low. "You wanna be Richard Rabbit?" she asks Oliver. "You want me to be Sweetheart?"

Oliver seems to hold his breath, then crawls out. "Don't forget you have to cover me up then because I'm a baby Richard that was just borned," he says. They stand and Reeny holds Oliver's hand. She leads him slowly to the doll corner. Of such is the pathway to redemption.

The next day, Reeny tells me she is doing a story for Oliver. "Once there was a rabbit Sweetheart and a baby Richard. He didn't have a mother so Sweetheart was his mother. And also his sister. Then he cried and cried because he was tired so she put him down to sleep and in the morning he was a prince."

When we are ready to act out our stories, Reeny takes Oliver by the hand and brings him to the rug. "We're doing the Sweetheart story," she says. "Wait till it's our turn, okay?"

Something tells me there may be some disappointments ahead for Reeny. Having forgiven Oliver for yesterday's rather scary incident, she now seems to feel a new sense of responsibility toward him. All morning she has been bringing him things and asking him to play, most of which he has ignored or said no to, preferring to draw instead. Now, however, she has put herself in charge of Oliver, or at least has organized his rabbits into a very different sort of story. Perhaps she has forgotten that Oliver would never change Richard into a prince; his characters remain the same always.

"Your story, Reeny," I call out, and she pulls Oliver with her to the center of the rug. "This is a good story," she tells him, "'cause you turn into a prince." As I begin to read, Oliver emits a low hum that quickly changes to a loud buzzing noise. He covers his ears and closes his eyes, and the buzzing becomes a roar. Bewildered, Reeny yells at him to stop, but he will not cease until I go to him and hold him in my arms. The story is done.

"Why he won't let me do my story?" Reeny asks me, when Oliver has returned to his corner table.

"I guess he just can't let someone else have Sweetheart and Richard," I say. "You can play it in the doll corner, but you can't write it down. Do you mind very much, Reeny?"

Reeny stares at Oliver, whose marker is moving faster across the page than I've ever seen. "Well, he can't be like Leo Lionni then! Not if that's the way he hasta be!"

"Oliver might change as he gets older," I say, but Reeny takes no comfort from this possibility. Clearly, it is easier to forgive some people than to remake them in your own image.

Later, at lunch, Reeny still ponders the Oliver enigma. "Now he's reminding me of that book about the mice with those big masks," she says, pointing to our most recently painted poster, *The Greentail Mouse.*

"Which part does he remind you of?" I ask.

"About the scary masks—what's that holiday?"

"Mardi Gras."

"Oh, yeah. They keep on those big scary masks so long they even scaring their own self and they forgetted they're just little mice. So then a little mouse comes and he don't—doesn't have a mask on, so they think he must be a giant 'cause he's the same size as they is."

"And Oliver?"

"Well, see, he forgets he's only a little boy in this room 'cause he keeps thinking he lives in another place. So that scares him."

Going Fishing

I can tell right away that Reeny's father is a confident story-teller, but today his patience will be strained. "This story is about a fishing trip I took with my father," Mr. Willens begins. "We had to drive a long way to my grandfather's farm in Mississippi. Well, actually, my grandmother's farm. My grandfather was in heaven."

"Why is your grandfather in heaven?"

"He passed away a long time ago. Anyway, we drove through Missouri and Arkansas and finally we got to a place called Yazoo—"

"He's dead?"

"Yes. Now, I kept saying, 'When we gonna get there, Daddy?' and he kept saying, 'In a little while, son.'"

"How did he die? Was he shotted?"

"No, he had a heart attack. His heart stopped working. Well, finally we got there, way out in the country, and the first thing I saw was a big, black pot—"

"If your heart stops working, if your heart attacks you, you're really dead."

"Sometimes people do get sick with respect to their hearts, children, and then they go to the hospital for help. Anyway, I said, 'Grandma, what's that big pot for? See, it was right there in the front yard.' And she told me, 'You'll find out later tonight,' so we all—"

"If your heart and your head both attacks you, and you're shot, you really are the most dead of all."

Mr. Willens takes a deep breath. "Okay, but this was natural, okay? So we went fishing, right? We had all the—"

"You'd be dead more from the head than from the heart 'cause in your head is your brain!"

"We had a long pole and a long string. Have any of you ever gone fishing before?"

"I never went fishing 'cause my dad knows it's poison fish, that's why."

"Well, in some waters. But not when I was a child." Mr. Willens looks at me, raising his eyebrows.

"Mr. Willens," I call out, "did your dad let you hold the pole?"

He flashes me a smile. "That's just it. They didn't fish with a pole. They took the long string and tied more strings to it, and each string had a hook at the bottom. Then they took the string on a little rowboat and rowed to the other side of the lake and tied it to a tree. Then they came back and took the other end and tied it to the pole. Then we left.

"I said to my dad, 'This isn't fun, we're not fishing with a pole.' But he said, 'When we come back, wait till you see how many fish will be waiting for us.' Later on that night we went back and you never saw so many fish. They needed all of us, me and my brothers and my cousins and uncles and aunts and my dad, to pull the fish in. We took the fish back and the grownups cleaned the fish while the children played."

"Daddy, was the big black pot still there?"

"Glad you remembered, honey. They started a big fire under the black pot and—oh, hi there, Oliver. Are you listening to my fishing story?"

Oliver comes up close. "If they shoot you then you have to be dead," he says.

"That's sometimes true, Oliver," Mr. Willens says gently. "You all don't need to worry about that sort of thing. No one will ever shoot you." Reeny climbs up on her father's lap while he finishes his story. "Then they put grease in the pot and it started boiling in the hot pot and they dropped in all the fish we caught. Oh boy, what a meal! We had corn bread and fresh greens and corn on the cob and all the fish we could eat."

"Mr. Willens, Mr. Willens, I'm sorry," Bruce says.

"About what, son?"

"That your grandpa died. I'm sorry he got sick and he died."

"Why thank you, Bruce. That's real nice of you to say that."

The Easy Tree

Perhaps all paths this year do lead to Leo Lionni. The day after her father's story, Reeny asks, "How come no one dies?" She points to our Leo Lionni bookshelf.

"Yeah they do," Bruce calls from his checkers game with Walter. "All those little red fish got ate by the big tuna."

"I mean like a mother or a father, like in Cinderella, or a grandfather."

"Are you remembering your father's story, that he told us his grandfather died?" I ask.

"I'm remembering about Jenny's mother," Reeny says. "Will they tell us about that?"

"I doubt it, Reeny. Unless someone asks."

Jenny's father and grandmother are coming today. "Not my mother," Jenny reminded us. She has told us about her mother's death many times. She is willing to repeat the story as often as she is asked and will bring the subject up on her own when she wants to talk about her mother. "I was two years old," she'll say. "My mother had cancer. That means she was very,

very sick. Sometimes I can't remember her face so I get her picture and look at it."

Mr. Bergen and his mother arrive after lunch. I feel we are entering a three-generational novel, beginning with Jenny's memories and going backward in time. Leo Lionni cannot supply such stories for us. We need real people, real family members to tell us this part of who we are.

"When I was your age," Mr. Bergen begins, "we had a tree in our little town called 'the easy tree.' That was because everyone in town could climb it, even little children. Then one day I wasn't careful enough and I fell from its lowest branch. I was bruised all over, but my brother said, "Don't tell anyone, okay? We'll say you fell off your bike. Because if you tell them, then we won't have a tree to call the easy tree anymore.""

The children smile at Mr. Bergen. In some way, each one understands that there must always be an easy tree; one cannot give up hope. The elderly Mrs. Bergen looks warmly at her son. "John, you never told me that story. I didn't know you fell out of the easy tree."

"Should Daddy have told you?" Jenny asks her grandmother. Everyone waits for the answer; this is not the sort of question the children expect in the classroom. But Mrs. Bergen replies comfortably. "Well, your dad trusted his brother to know what was best. Now, children, my story is about a place with no easy tree. When I was little we lived on a farm in Nova Scotia. The ground was so hard you could hardly grow anything. But we were lucky. We had a cow that always gave milk, the sweetest milk ever tasted."

"Was that the easy tree?" Reeny asks.

Mrs. Bergen looks deeply into Reeny's face. "Come up here, child. Let me give you a hug, may I? You just gave me something good to think about. Our good dependable cow, she certainly was our easy tree. You're absolutely right."

While Mrs. Bergen finishes her story, in which the cow is lost and then found in the middle of a frozen pond, unable to get off, I can't help wondering if Reeny's ability to use the easy tree as metaphor is due in part to the practice we've had in analyzing Leo Lionni.

Yet isn't it more likely the other way around? That is, the Leo Lionni stories and the easy-tree stories work so well because the children come to school knowing how to think about such matters. We need only to give them the proper *context* in which to demonstrate and fine-tune their natural gifts.

There are, of course, certain contexts each child brings independently. "Was your cow brown?" Reeny asks.

Mrs. Bergen laughs. "Well, yes, mostly brown she was at that. We called her Cocoa. Why do you ask, Reeny?"

"Because she's a easy-tree cow. Brown is easy."

Mr. McMouse

"This is no easy tree," I say after reading our latest Leo Lionni book, *Mr. McMouse*. With its 1992 publishing date, it may be his most recent book.

"Let's begin again," I suggest, turning back to the first page, where a mouse named Timothy stands looking at himself in the mirror, feeling quite happy. ("'What a good-looking city mouse I am!' he thought.") But one page later his world falls apart. There he is again, in front of the same mirror, wearing a black Homburg and morning coat, unrecognizable to himself and presumably to us. ("He jumped back, let out a shriek, and ran for his life.")

"I don't get it," Reeny says, shaking her head. "Can someone else get in your mirror?"

"It hasta be a dream," Cory decides. "Or else he bought some clothes and fell asleep in them and when he wakes up he looks in the mirror and he forgets he has new clothes on."

"Maybe it's Halloween," Anita says, "and he put on a costume and scared hisself."

Reeny listens to the growing number of explanations without committing herself. She seems more interested in the idea that *Mr. McMouse* is a book she does not understand. For the first time she asks for my opinion.

"I'm not at all sure. In a way, Timothy reminds me of Pezzettino, wondering 'Who am I?' or maybe of Little Blue and Little Yellow when they suddenly turn green and no one recognizes them. But, of course, Timothy can't even remember his own name."

("Suddenly the weeds parted, and a little field mouse stepped boldly forward. 'Hello,' she said, 'I'm Spinny. What's your name?' 'I am . . . I am . . . ,' mumbled Timothy, confused. The field mice stared at him. Spinny smiled. 'Never mind,' she said. 'I'll give you a name: Mister McMouse!'")

The story has a happy ending, with Timothy saving the field mice from a cat, but the meaning of the mirror scene remains obscure. "It's a magic mirror," Jenny says. "When you look in it you could be dressed in a different way."

The author has presented a Kafkaesque situation in which our hero has suddenly lost his image, his name, his entire identity, and neither he nor we know why. When Tico's golden wings appear we know that a wishing bird has intervened. But Timothy's metamorphosis comes without explanation—unless, of course, we are to infer that, as a city mouse, he has lived so long with people that he now sees himself as a person. Since he doesn't know how people think or feel, he is left without even a name to call his own.

My thoughts go off in another direction. If the inchworm represents Leo Lionni escaping from the advertising profession, does the new book tell us that perhaps, one day, the author woke up in New York City and realized he had become someone else, someone unrecognizable, someone who needed to return home in order to look for himself again?

"Does Timothy ever remember his own name?" several children want to know.

"The book doesn't tell us," I say. "I wondered about that too."

"Yes, he *does* remember," Jenny assures us, "because he has a friend now. Spinny is his friend so he has to know his name."

What a splendid notion! It is through the mirror of friendship that you find yourself when you are lost. The children do not recognize themselves in the school mirror until a friend comes along, someone who can be trusted to see them as they wish to be seen. Walter did not tell us his real name until Reeny connected him to Pezzettino. But no, she was his friend long before she identified him as an artist; she needed no proof of his special talents.

"Walter," I ask, "when you first came to our classroom you didn't know anyone. When did you find a friend?"

Though surprised by my question, he is eager to answer. "First I looked people is playing same in Warsaw. So then playing is—they—I and *they* is playing. Now we friends can be. Ha!" He claps his hands and laughs.

I gaze at the children, who join Walter in his laughter. These are my friends too. They know my real name. And what if the mirror that holds my truest reflection is the one that hangs on the classroom wall? When I no longer hear the name "teacher" will I be left with no name at all?

Family Discussion

When Reeny's grandmother picks her up after school I hand her *Mr. McMouse*. "Will you read this book, Ettie, and tell me what you make of it? We're having trouble with the mirror scene. This is no *Swimmy*, I can tell you."

Miss Ettie calls me that evening after dinner. "Vivian, my first thought was, this is what happens to colored folks who hang out with too many white people. They lose their image."

"That was your *first* thought. And then . . . ?"

"Well, then I talked about it with Reeny and she did not agree with me at all. She said, 'Grandma, if you have friends it's okay.' So then we all talked about the book at dinner. Reeny told us that Walter is the only boy who speaks Polish, but he has lots of friends and he's happy. Then she went on, nonstop, about Cory and Jenny and Bruce and Frederick and Tico and Oliver until we couldn't tell who was in a book and who was real. But, for her, the subject is *friendship*, plain and simple. Friendship is everything."

"What did her parents make of Timothy and the mirror?"

"Steve said, 'Every once in a while, I look in the mirror when I'm shaving and I don't know myself. Especially after I've gone and done something mean to someone.' And then my daughter came up with this: Maybe Timothy wasn't even his real name. Maybe it was given to him by humans, and he didn't have mouse friends in the city to call him by his real name. So he had to get back to his own kind in order to know himself." *Social context and need for friends/comm*

"That was a pretty good discussion, Ettie."

"Wait, it wasn't over. While we were cleaning up, Reeny said, 'That mouse has to dream himself a new name.' And then, as if it was part of the same subject, she said, 'Brown Baby is going to be in my story tomorrow, in my notebook.'"

"Who is Brown Baby?"

"Her imaginary playmate. He *never* leaves home! Why now? It feels funny knowing she's going to do this."

"Maybe she'll change her mind," I suggest.

"Could be. But my Reeny is someone who keeps thinking of new angles. You know what she told me at bedtime? She said, 'Grandma, you forgot something about Swimmy. He was the leader of red fish. *Red* fish. That means a black fish could be the leader of another color fish.'"

Brown Baby

Why *does* Reeny want us to know about Brown Baby? Does this sudden impulse have anything to do with the *Mr. McMouse* discussion at home? "Once there was Brown Baby," she dictates the next day, looking around as if to judge our reactions, "and he decided not to go to school with the little girl. So he said, 'I'm playing by my own self today.' So he walked all around the school and he slided down the slide and he smelled the flowers. And then the little girl carried him home."

"Does Brown Baby live in your house?" Cory asks.

"Brown Baby—um, he does come from my house. But now he comes from my head. Uh, yeah, he does live in my house."

When Reeny next brings me her notebook she has printed "Chapter 1" and "Chapter 2" at the top of consecutive pages. "I'm doing a chapter book," she says, "like *Charlotte's Web.*" The second installment of her story is preceded by "BB" for Brown Baby. "Then Brown Baby saw Tico and he was crying because his friends didn't like him any more. But Brown Baby liked his wings that was golden. So they played until the little girl came out and then Tico went back into his book. And she took Brown Baby home."

"Is Brown Baby a person?" Jenny asks. "Does he have a mother?"

"His mother is dead. And also his father."

A day later, Chapter 3: "Nobody can see Brown Baby, only the little girl and Tico can. Then Frederick wants to play with Brown Baby, but Leo Lionni won't let him come out of the book. 'Come in, huh, come in, huh, Brown Baby come in!' But Brown Baby said no."

Reeny begins decorating the pages of her notebook in Oliver style, drawing rows of figures that appear to be doing things together, connected in a story of some kind, though perhaps not the Brown Baby story.

"Which one is Brown Baby?" Cory asks. "Did you draw Brown Baby?" Reeny shakes her head but offers no explanation.

Chapter 4: "Tico comes out every day to play with Brown Baby. Then Brown Baby sat on Tico's back and they flied up to the sky. They could see the whole of the school. The little girl waved at them in the window. But the others wasn't at the window."

I've seldom seen Reeny so perplexed. She wants to tell us something about this intimate fantasy of hers yet fears our intrusions. She'll neither draw Brown Baby nor let anyone pretend to be him. Thus we are allowed to hear the stories, but they are not to be acted out or reproduced in any way.

The children, however, are now in the habit of questioning everything that concerns Leo Lionni. "How come no one sees the empty space in the book when Tico flies out?" But they especially want to know "Why can't Frederick come out, and Tico is allowed to go into the playground and play with Brown Baby?" This seems unfair, they all agree.

Walter has a theory. "Frederick not go in playground because cat is there." But Bruce dismisses the notion. "No way! A cat can't eat someone from a book."

Every new set of questions produces a response in Reeny's narrative. "Tico flied back in the window but no one can see him. He told Frederick to get on his back because he'll be invisible. So Frederick came out to play with Brown Baby."

At this point something happens to upset the equilibrium: Cory decides to play Brown Baby in the doll corner. "I'll be the little girl," she says, "And you're Brown Baby, okay? I'm your mommy."

To Cory's dismay, Reeny runs out of the doll corner. "I got to do my story!" she shouts, pushing her notebook at me. "Tico and Frederick got lost. The little girl looked in the books and it was empty. Come back, come back, and so they flied back into the book and she closed the cover. Goodbye! Come home, Brown Baby! And they played until the cock crows. The end."

Abruptly we hear no more about Brown Baby. The story ceases; the ledger is balanced again between private fantasy and school reality. Perhaps Leo Lionni felt the same way when he finished *Mr. McMouse,* also rather hastily, I thought. "There," he may have said, "I was compelled to do that mirror scene, but I'll explain no further. I intend to leave everyone, including myself, in doubt as to what it means."

94

Until the
Cock Crows

Brown Baby is gone as suddenly as he appeared, but for some children the chapter stories are now a daily ritual. Even Walter has been caught up in the excitement of ending a story with "To be continued," letting the characters and plots repeat or contradict one another the next day, in a new chapter.

Walter's stories follow the adventures of Stanislaw and his cat Luiza, who continually chase a dog named Jakub. But the dog is clever and they always end up bumping their heads or falling down a hole, at which point Walter says, in a sing-song voice, "To be continued ha ha!"

"Are you telling a Jakub story today?" Reeny asks, sliding in next to Walter at the story table. He has become her storyteller of choice from among the children, and often he seems to be performing exclusively for her amusement.

"Listen, Reeny," he says, grinning. "Story of chapters. Once a time chapter is one and the end is coming. Until the cock crows. To be continued ha ha!"

Reeny laughs until she nearly falls off her chair, really or pretend I cannot tell, but Walter is encouraged to go on. He hands me his notebook again. "Two chapter!" he announces. "Then coming chapter two. Until the cock crows. The end ha ha ha!"

The children roar with delight when Walter's new dramatic opus is presented. He runs to the center of the rug twice, we all crow each time in our best rooster fashion, and then he returns to his place. It is minimalist theater, akin to his basic art form, the square. But beyond that, we realize he is making fun of his own chapter stories. Walter, it turns out, has quite a sophisticated sense of humor, though I did not know it.

Reeny and Cory are not as surprised as I am. "Like that other time, right, Walter?" Reeny says. What other time? How many other daily events escape my attention in the classroom? The children keep track of each other's footprints in a way no magnifying instrument of mine can ever accomplish. Perhaps, all along, it has been *I* who needed Leo Lionni to help me know the children and myself within a consistent and continual context.

The end of the school year approaches. The cock is crowing urgently, but his raucous call ends in a question mark. Then I hear Reeny humming to herself at the painting table, and I feel I can go on forever.

Not in school, of course. Like Brown Baby, I'll have to find adventures elsewhere. Reeny, Oliver, and Walter, Cory, Bruce, and the others will become *my* imaginary playmates. They'll talk to me inside the books I have yet to write and sing to me as I walk in the forest deeply to the little house in which, following Reeny's advice for Mr. McMouse, I too shall dream of a new name for myself.

"Grandma Ettie says you're not going to be a teacher any more," Reeny says. "What will you be?"

"It's hard to think about that, Reeny, since I'm still your teacher right now."

She whispers in my ear. "I'd most rather stay here with you and everybody next year."

She looks at me hopefully. Is it possible, she wonders. Can such dreams come true?

"Wouldn't that be lovely?" I whisper back. "But you know, you'll be ready for first grade."

"How about Leo Lionni?"

"We can think about him and read his books and draw his mice whenever we wish, Reeny. And write stories about him."

"Will you do that?" she asks me.

"Yes, I believe I will."

"Okay, then, me too." Reeny runs to the doll corner where Cory is waiting. The table is set, the scarves are pulled out, ready to be put on, and a new story is about to begin.

"What will you do with the Leo Lionni posters?" the children ask, noticing that Nisha and I have begun to remove certain items from the wall. "Don't take them down. They need to stay here," Jenny says. "Are you taking them down?"

Nisha and I look at each other. The children know that next year this will be her classroom; it is her decision to make. "I really haven't thought about this yet," she tells us, "but probably the new children will want to paint their own posters."

"Will they want to paint Leo Lionni posters?" Reeny asks.

"Maybe a different book they like better to paint," Walter says. "Maybe something else."

"There weren't this many posters last year," I recall. "The children painted a winter scene and then one in spring, with trees and flowers and birds. Oh, yes, there were some that had to do with airplanes and trains and, in fact, the city of Chicago. We had to turn the paper the long way to make the Sears Tower and the John Hancock building."

The children stare at me, realizing suddenly that another group of children, in this very room, concerned themselves with other matters. The information brings Reeny to her feet. She reaches out as if to touch the posters.

"Please can't we leave them up?" she urges. "Because otherwise they won't know what we did. The new children, they'll say, like, 'Who was in this room? We have to know who lived here!' That's what they're going to say. And then, see, after they get a good look at every poster and they say, 'Oh, what's this one called,' like that, and 'Tell us all the names of the children that did this fine work.' Okay, then, after that, let them paint their own posters. Because, see, how do you know? They might decide to do Leo Lionni!"

Nisha laughs. "That *will* be a nice thing to do on the first day of school. Yes, let's keep the posters up for now. The new children will want to know all about the people who painted these beautiful posters. I'll tell them the story of the year of Leo Lionni."

"And tell them about Tico," Reeny says.

"What shall I tell them about Tico?" asks Nisha.

Reeny speaks directly to me. "Tell them he *could* keep his gold wings. Tico should tell his friends, 'I just *like* to have these golden wings. Why can't you still be my friends? It's only golden wings. What's so wrong about that?'"

"If he had said that," I ask Reeny, "what would his friends have said?"

"Well, probably, they would say, 'I won't be your friend because you have golden wings.' But, see, like then Tico says, 'Yes, you could too be my friend. I just don't want to give up my wings because I like them, because they look pretty. I'm not saying I look prettier than you. But I'm thinking, why don't you stay and we'll *talk* about it. Don't fly away. See, we can keep talking about it, okay?'"

Books by Leo Lionni

The following are the Leo Lionni books referred to in the text.

Alexander and the Wind-Up Mouse. New York: Pantheon, 1969.

The Biggest House in the World. New York: Pantheon, 1968.

Cornelius. New York: Pantheon, 1983.

Fish Is Fish. New York: Pantheon, 1970.

Frederick. New York: Pantheon, 1967.

Geraldine the Music Mouse. New York: Pantheon, 1979.

The Greentail Mouse. New York: Pantheon, 1973.

In the Rabbitgarden. New York: Pantheon, 1975.

Inch by Inch. New York: Obolensky, 1960.

Little Blue and Little Yellow. New York: McDowell Obolensky, 1959.

Mr. McMouse. New York: Alfred A. Knopf, 1992.

Pezzettino. New York: Pantheon, 1975.

Swimmy. New York: Pantheon, 1967.

Tico and the Golden Wings. New York: Pantheon, 1964.